THE **TESTING** SERIES

DOTS CONCENTRATION
TESTS

THE **TESTING** SERIES

expert advice on test preparation

Orders: Please contact How2become Ltd, Suite 2, 50 Churchill Square Business Centre, Kings Hill, Kent ME19 4YU.

Telephone: (44) 0845 643 1299 - Lines are open Monday to Friday 9am until 5pm. Fax: (44) 01732 525965. You can also order via the e mail address info@how2become.co.uk and at Gardners.com.

ISBN: 9781907558993

First published 2012

Typeset for How2become Ltd by Molly Hill, Canada.

Printed in Great Britain for How2become Ltd by Bell & Bain Ltd, 303 Burnfield Road, Thornliebank, Glasgow G46 7UQ.

CONTENTS

DOTS CONCENTRATION TESTS

INTRODUCTION

Dear Sir/Madam,

Welcome to your new guide Dots Concentration Tests (DCT). This guide has been designed to help you prepare for the concentration tests that will form part of the Trainee Train Driver selection process. We feel certain that you will find the guide an invaluable asset for helping you obtain one of the most sought after careers available.

The Train Driver selection process is not easy. It is comprehensive, relatively drawn out and highly competitive. In fact, on average there are between 300 and 400 applicants for every vacancy. Coupled with the fact that Train Operating Companies rarely advertise posts, this makes it an even harder job to obtain. However, do not let this put you off, as many of the applicants who do apply are grossly under prepared, and they normally fail as a result. You must prepare fully if you are to pass the selection process and be offered a position as a Trainee Train Driver. The majority of Train Operating Companies (TOCs) are both professional and meticulous in how they run their assessment centres, and you should find the process an enjoyable one. We hope that you enjoy the testing guide and we wish you all the best in your pursuit of becoming a Train Driver.

If you would like any further assistance with the selection process then we offer the following products and training courses via the website www.how2become.com.

- How to become a Train Driver book
- How to pass the Train Driver interview DVD
- 1 Day intensive Train Driver course at the following website

WWW.TRAINDRIVERCOURSE.CO.UK

Finally, you won't achieve much in life without hard work, determination and perseverance. Work hard, stay focused and be what you want!

Good luck and best wishes,

The how2become team

The How2become Team

PREFACE BY AUTHOR RICHARD MCMUNN

Before I get into the guide and teach you how to prepare for the Dots Concentration Test, it is important that I explain a little bit about my background and why I am qualified to help you succeed.

I joined the Royal Navy soon after leaving school and spent four fabulous years in the Fleet Air Arm branch onboard HMS Invincible. It had always been my dream to become a Firefighter and I only ever intended staying in the Royal Navy for the minimum amount of time. At the age of 21 I left the Royal Navy and joined Kent Fire and Rescue Service. Over the next 17 years I had an amazing career with a fantastic organisation. During that time I was heavily involved in training and recruitment, often sitting on interview panels and marking application forms for those people who wanted to become Firefighters. I also worked very hard and rose to the rank of Station Manager. I passed numerous assessment centres during my time in the job and I estimate that I was successful at over 95% of interviews I attended.

The reason for my success was not because I am special in anyway, or that I have lots of educational qualifications, because I don't! In the build up to every job application or promotion I always prepared myself thoroughly. I found a formula that worked and I always stuck to it.

Over the past few years I have taught many people how to pass the selection process for becoming a Trainee Train Driver, both through guides like this one and also during my one day intensive training course at www.traindrivercourse.co.uk.

Each and every one of the students who attends my course is determined to pass, and that is what you will need to do too if you are to be successful. As you are probably aware many people want to become Train Drivers. As a result of this, the competition is fierce. However, the vast majority of people who do apply will submit poor application forms or they will do very little to prepare for the assessment centre and the interviews. As a result, they will fail.

The way to pass the selection process is to embark on a comprehensive period of intense preparation. I would urge you to use an action plan during your preparation. This will allow you to focus your mind on exactly what you need to do in order to pass. For example, if it has been many years since you last attended an interview, then you will probably have a lot of work to do in this area. If it has been many years since you last sat a test, then you may have to work very hard in order to pass the psychometric tests that form part of the assessment centre. The point I am making here, is that it is within your power to improve on your weak areas. If you use an action plan then you are far more likely to achieve your goals.

I use action plans in just about every element of my work. Action plans work simply because they focus your mind on what needs to be done. Once you have created your action plan, stick it in a prominent position such as your fridge door. This will act as a reminder of the work that you need to do in order to prepare properly for selection. Your action plan might look something like this:

MY WEEKLY ACTION PLAN FOR PREPARING FOR TRAIN DRIVER SELECTION

Monday	Tuesday	Wednesday	Thursday	Friday
Research into the TOC I am applying for. Includes reading recruitment literature and visiting websites.	60 minute Interview preparation including preparing my responses to questions.	Obtain application form and read recruitment literature and application form guidance notes.	Research into the TOC I am applying for. Includes reading recruitment literature and visiting websites.	60 minute mock interview with a friend or relative.
60 minutes preparation on Mechanical Comprehension tests and Assessing Information.	30 minute Dots Concentration test preparation.	45 minute fast reaction preparation using 'Bop it' toy.	60 minutes preparation on Mechanical Comprehension tests and Assessing Information.	30 minute Dots Concentration test preparation.
20 minute jog or brisk walk.	30 minutes gym work.	20 minutes reading about the role of a Train Driver.	20 minute jog or brisk walk.	30 minutes gym work.

Note: Saturday and Sunday, rest days.

The above sample action plan is just a simple example of what you may wish to include as part of your preparation for the Train Driver selection process. Your action plan will very much depend on your strengths and weaknesses and at which stage of selection you are.

Finally, it is very important that you believe in your own abilities. It does not matter if you have no qualifications. It does not matter if you have no knowledge yet of the role of a Train Driver. What does matter is self belief, self discipline and a genuine desire to improve and become successful.

Enjoy the testing guide and then set out on a period of intense preparation!

Best wishes,
Richard McMunn

DOTS CONCENTRATION TESTS

DISCLAIMER

Every effort has been made to ensure that the information contained within this guide is accurate at the time of publication. How2become Ltd are not responsible for anyone failing any part of any selection process as a result of the information contained within this guide. How2become Ltd and their authors cannot accept any responsibility for any errors or omissions within this guide, however caused. No responsibility for loss or damage occasioned by any person acting, or refraining from action, as a result of the material in this publication can be accepted by How2become Ltd.

The information within this guide does not represent the views of any third party service or organisation.

DOTS CONCENTRATION TESTS

ABOUT THE DOTS CONCENTRATION TEST

The Dots Concentration Test is an assessment that specifically assesses your level of concentration, and is one of the hardest parts of the assessment process. It is the one test that most people fail and this is mainly due to a lack of preparation. Many candidates turn up to take the test without any prior knowledge of how the test works and what is expected of them.

The test is designed to assess your ability to concentrate whilst performing tasks at high speed. The test will be carried out either with a pen and paper, or a computer and a computer screen. Whichever test you undertake, you will be presented with five pages or screens that each contains 25 columns. Each of the columns contains boxes with patterns of dots which are either in groups of 2, 3, 4, 5 or 6. Your task is to work quickly and accurately through each column, from left to right, identifying boxes of **4 dots** only.

You are allowed two minutes only per sheet and, once the two minutes are up, you are told to move onto the next page regardless of whether you have completed it or not. I can confidently say that you will not complete each page in the allotted two minutes per sheet, simply because there are too many groups of dots to work through!

The test requires ten minutes of solid concentration.

DOTS CONCENTRATION TESTS

Take a look at the following row of dots:

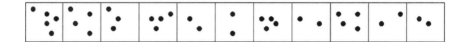

You will notice that the 2nd, 4th, 7th and 9th boxes each contain 4 dots. If you were taking the paper and pencil based version of the test, you would mark the boxes that contain 4 dots as follows:

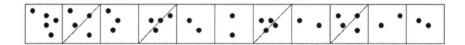

You will notice that I have placed a single diagonal line through each of the boxes that contains 4 dots.

If you are required to undertake a computer based version of the test, then you will be required to use the keys on the keyboard as follows:

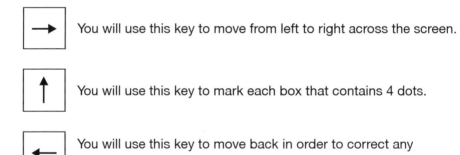

You will use this key to move from left to right across the screen.

You will use this key to mark each box that contains 4 dots.

You will use this key to move back in order to correct any mistakes.

It is crucial that you aim for accuracy as well as speed. You will lose marks for incorrect answers; therefore, you will need to work hard on improving your concentration levels. You will find that during the first couple of sheets your concentration levels will be good; however, after a few minutes it will become harder to concentrate. Many people talk about seeing a 'mass of dots' after the third sheet and they find it hard to concentrate as a result. I have deliberately supplied you with twenty sample tests, each containing five sheets of dots. By the end of the guide you should notice that your tests improve greatly.

If you wish to try out the Dots Concentration Tests online, please go to:

WWW.TRAINDRIVERTESTS.CO.UK

On the following pages I have provided you with ten sample concentration tests as an introduction. During the first set of five concentration tests you are required to locate specific letters and/or numbers that are contained within rows and columns. Full instructions are provided at the start of each test.

During the second set of five Dots Concentration tests, you will be required to search for groups of 4 dots in rows and columns of boxes. Once again, full instructions are provided.

Please note: these initial introductory tests are designed to provide you with a 'feel' that closely resembles the concentration assessments. Treat them as a practice guidance only. Please make sure you have a stopwatch or watch available to monitor your time.

DOTS CONCENTRATION TESTS

SAMPLE CONCENTRATION TEST 1

Cross out the letter 'R' (upper case) in each row. Write down the total number that you cross out in each row in the box provided at the end of each row. You have 60 seconds to complete the test.

#																
1.	Q	r	R	g	y	U	h	J	R	j	R	k	L	B	n	3 1
2.	R	R	R	v	B	n	M	U	u	d	f	O	p	T	R	4
3.	C	x	X	F	R	G	t	p	A	R	f	V	R	y	U	3
4.	Q	R	R	t	G	N	H	J	r	r	F	P	F	R	r	3
5.	Q	a	Z	x	R	t	I	o	M	B	R	D	x	A	S	1 x
6.	R	s	a	A	e	E	R	C	Y	U	r	j	P	o	R	3
7.	T	R	r	P	F	r	S	N	b	V	c	F	F	R	R	3
8.	G	v	R	r	R	y	R	P	R	r	D	e	E	R	F	5
9.	T	R	K	P	o	u	b	g	t	m	R	r	X	r	R	3
10.	C	B	n	h	j	Y	I	p	R	R	R	r	R	C	d	4
11.	R	R	r	Y	u	B	v	M	n	h	K	j	R	E	R	4
12.	A	W	r	E	R	f	p	U	I	H	R	y	U	B	R	3
13.	R	r	Q	q	B	G	R	t	Q	w	E	F	T	y	R	3
14.	T	R	A	I	N	D	P	I	V	E	R	D	T	y	S	2
15.	d	x	z	Z	R	n	K	i	i	R	r	R	O	p	o	3
16.	Q	R	r	E	D	D	e	w	K	i	I	O	P	R	R	3
17	H	O	w	B	e	E	R	r	R	R	V	R	H	j	R	5
18.	K	j	u	U	Y	i	Y	r	R	R	D	X	z	q	Q	2
19.	P	y	g	h	j	I	r	t	r	e	R	e	R	q	Z	2
20.	B	h	B	h	r	r	R	r	N	B	H	y	Y	R	F	2

SAMPLE CONCENTRATION TEST 2

Cross out the letter 'o' (lower case). Write down the total number that you cross out in each row in the box provided at the end of each row. You have 60 seconds to complete the test.

1.	o	O	t	Q	w	q	O	o	A	B	u	U	o	o	O	4
2.	O	o	g	Y	t	B	c	C	c	O	o	o	o	D	w	4
3.	B	o	O	g	a	s	S	q	Q	t	Q	q	O	o	G	2
4.	I	L	N	h	U	u	O	o	H	y	t	R	o	O	o	3
5.	G	V	v	R	t	Y	o	o	P	i	O	O	o	O	R	3
6.	G	t	y	U	J	P	p	O	o	D	d	O	o	S	Q	2
7.	O	o	O	o	o	o	Y	t	Y	q	Q	q	o	c	c	5
8.	I	u	V	c	c	F	r	d	w	H	y	h	u	o	o	1
9.	Y	o	o	U	o	O	O	y	D	e	q	A	q	O	o	4
10.	R	r	t	o	u	y	G	b	t	r	e	o	o	o	P	4
11.	o	O	c	o	d	d	D	O	c	c	O	o	o	d	R	4
12.	B	v	c	f	R	o	y	f	D	r	d	r	a	A	a	1
13.	F	t	t	t	d	r	e	o	o	p	u	o	Q	t	r	3
14.	F	g	r	t	y	N	H	N	h	o	p	O	o	I	y	2
15.	T	r	e	d	w	o	u	i	y	F	c	r	D	e	W	1
16.	o	o	O	o	p	O	u	i	S	t	d	r	s	S	O	3
17.	I	o	O	A	a	a	c	C	c	g	o	o	o	R	t	4
18.	G	g	g	g	o	t	f	d	r	t	u	u	o	o	j	3
19.	Q	c	v	b	g	t	y	u	O	o	O	o	G	y	c	2
20.	K	I	o	i	u	y	t	r	e	o	u	y	o	j	h	3

DOTS CONCENTRATION TESTS

SAMPLE CONCENTRATION TEST 3

Cross out the letters 'w' (lower case) and 'V' (upper case). Search for both of these letters at the same time. Write down the total combined number that you cross out in each row in the box provided at the end of each row. You have 60 seconds to complete the test.

1.	v	W	w	V	e	w	h	j	U	i	X	x	W	w	v	4
2.	V	u	U	w	G	t	y	u	W	w	V	v	W	o	o	4
3.	W	W	V	V	v	v	w	w	y	u	i	p	v	W	W	4
4.	V	g	h	j	K	O	p	t	Y	V	v	W	W	w	V	8
5.	Y	U	u	u	v	v	W	M	m	w	e	V	v	N	n	2
6.	q	q	Q	G	g	H	Y	u	i	R	T	y	V	w	v	1
7.	V	y	u	Y	u	o	p	N	h	j	W	w	V	V	v	4
8.	t	y	m	k	m	N	b	C	x	W	w	V	v	b	v	2
9.	O	o	V	v	f	g	h	j	k	n	h	N	h	V	X	2
10.	T	V	v	X	c	d	W	w	W	v	V	v	f	r	p	3
11.	V	V	v	w	W	w	v	V	v	W	w	g	y	Y	v	5
12.	R	t	y	u	i	B	g	v	f	r	D	r	Q	w	W	1
13.	R	t	y	V	c	V	c	v	f	r	W	w	W	w	V	
14.	G	y	u	i	O	p	R	t	y	E	w	V	V	v	W	
15.	Y	Y	y	Y	X	v	W	W	w	w	r	t	y	u	v	
16.	W	w	w	v	t	u	i	n	h	v	V	w	W	w	f	
17.	r	t	y	y	u	i	V	b	n	h	g	w	w	W	w	
18.	i	o	q	w	S	S	X	W	V	Z	z	V	v	W	y	
19.	P	o	Y	u	i	V	v	X	w	W	w	R	t	R	y	
20.	y	u	V	x	s	t	Y	u	y	W	w	C	d	V	w	

SAMPLE CONCENTRATION TEST 4

Cross out the number 8 and the letter 'b' (lower case). Search for both letter and number at the same time. Write down the total combined number that you cross out in each row in the box provided at the end of each row. You have 60 seconds to complete the test.

1.	8	B	8	V	v	W	q	P	p	r	g	B	b	8	u	
2.	B	b	R	r	r	y	U	i	8	8	B	B	b	g	G	
3.	j	u	p	P	b	v	f	r	B	b	w	3	6	7	R	
4.	8	3	2	h	y	U	x	W	w	v	x	v	b	B	8	
5.	f	G	g	B	p	h	b	b	b	B	B	8	8	5	3	
6.	y	u	U	7	6	5	8	e	r	d	r	w	8	B	b	
7.	o	O	o	P	7	8	5	b	3	8	3	R	r	S	I	
8.	B	b	3	8	B	B	b	h	h	V	c	b	B	7	1	
9.	1	3	c	V	f	I	u	y	t	r	B	b	8	8	8	
10.	y	B	b	8	4	3	3	3	X	x	x	f	F	r	t	
11.	Q	q	H	b	B	b	8	B	6	3	3	2	u	B	b	
12.	G	G	g	B	b	8	3	8	3	D	d	D	I	P	p	
13.	G	b	b	8	8	6	5	4	0	L	o	P	p	P	B	
14	3	B	b	8	3	B	B	b	3	E	e	3	8	4	P	
15.	t	Y	y	D	e	e	D	f	g	W	8	8	P	P	B	
16.	C	C	b	n	B	8	B	8	B	b	8	3	9	3	9	
17.	6	6	b	B	8	8	d	k	I	p	o	U	S	y	Y	
18.	P	p	8	F	d	D	c	C	8	B	b	8	f	F	f	
19.	8	8	C	f	z	s	W	w	R	r	T	8	3	B	b	
20.	H	y	y	b	B	8	8	8	H	H	h	D	r	e	W	

DOTS CONCENTRATION TESTS

SAMPLE CONCENTRATION TEST 5

Cross out the letter 'e' (lower case) and the number '3'. Search for both letter and number at the same time. Write down the number crossed out in the box provided at the end of each row. You have 60 seconds to complete the test.

1.	E	6	e	8	8	e	3	p	b	d	e	E	3	8	T	
2.	e	8	3	6	7	y	u	I	V	f	E	e	b	B	E	
3.	W	w	q	D	d	c	x	z	O	p	e	R	6	8	3	
4.	y	u	I	o	p	P	t	T	Y	e	E	3	8	6	F	
5.	g	B	4	3	2	7	8	3	e	E	3	4	E	e	3	
6.	e	3	3	e	E	d	W	q	h	j	K	8	7	N	9	
7.	3	e	E	8	B	8	3	e	E	k	K	3	e	8	7	
8.	f	C	x	b	g	t	T	r	6	8	3	4	X	d	e	
9.	3	3	3	b	8	b	e	3	E	3	8	3	4	0	1	
10.	e	E	j	H	g	b	3	E	e	3	w	b	V	v	E	
11.	8	3	B	v	C	f	v	e	8	4	3	3	3	e	v	
12.	6	7	8	v	c	D	f	3	7	8	6	E	e	e	V	
13.	e	3	e	3	E	8	E	3	e	E	3	2	8	G	g	
14.	7	y	h	n	g	f	d	e	E	4	E	e	3	D	d	
15	k	I	L	j	h	y	V	v	8	4	2	b	V	v	E	
16.	g	Y	y	i	9	8	7	0	3	O	o	v	V	v	e	
17.	8	2	B	b	v	e	W	e	r	5	5	R	r	e	V	
18.	3	e	E	e	3	4	b	V	v	e	W	w	q	A	a	
19.	5	e	3	V	f	r	6	5	4	e	e	E	e	3	E	
20.	e	E	e	R	3	4	2	1	3	E	e	h	G	f	d	

ANSWERS TO CONCENTRATION TESTS

Row #	TEST 1	TEST 2	TEST 3	TEST 4	TEST 5
1.	3	4	4	4	5
2.	4	4	4	4	3
3.	3	2	4	2	2
4.	3	3	4	3	2
5.	2	3	2	5	6
6.	3	2	2	3	4
7.	3	5	4	3	6
8.	5	2	2	4	2
9.	3	4	2	4	7
10.	4	4	3	2	4
11.	4	4	6	4	6
12.	3	1	1	3	3
13.	3	3	5	4	7
14.	2	2	3	4	3
15	3	1	2	2	0
16.	3	3	5	5	2
17.	5	4	4	3	3
18.	2	3	3	4	5
19.	2	2	3	4	6
20.	2	3	4	4	5

Check through your answers carefully and go back to check over the ones you got wrong.

Now move onto the next set of five Dots Concentration tests which are similar to the actual test itself.

SAMPLE DOTS CONCENTRATION TEST 1

Place a diagonal line across each box that contains 4 dots only. You have 60 seconds to complete the test.

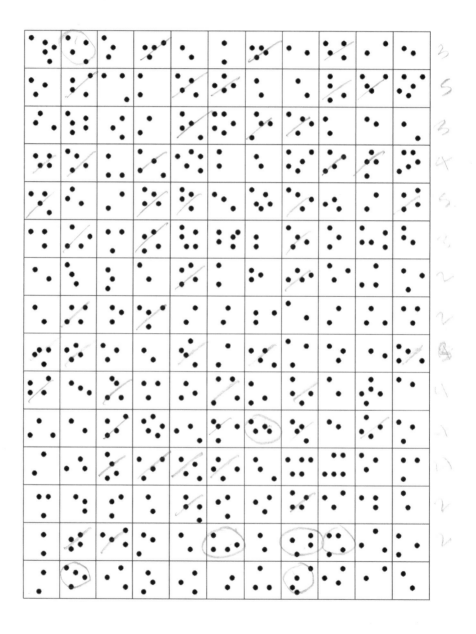

SAMPLE DOTS CONCENTRATION TEST 2

Place a diagonal line across each box that contains 4 dots only. You have 60 seconds to complete the test.

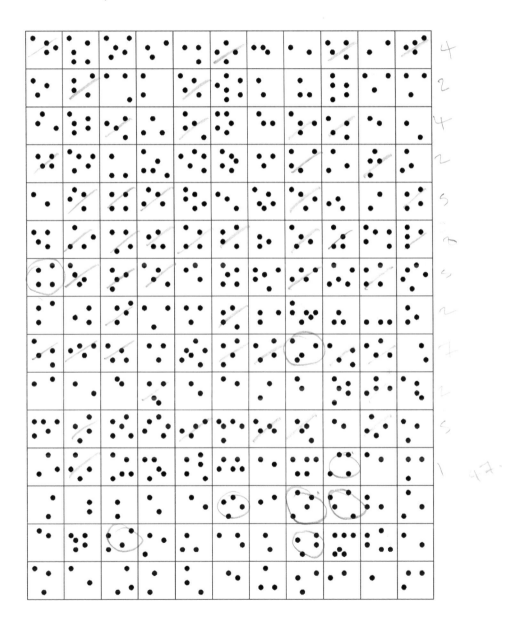

SAMPLE DOTS CONCENTRATION TEST 3

Place a diagonal line across each box that contains 4 dots only. You have 60 seconds to complete the test.

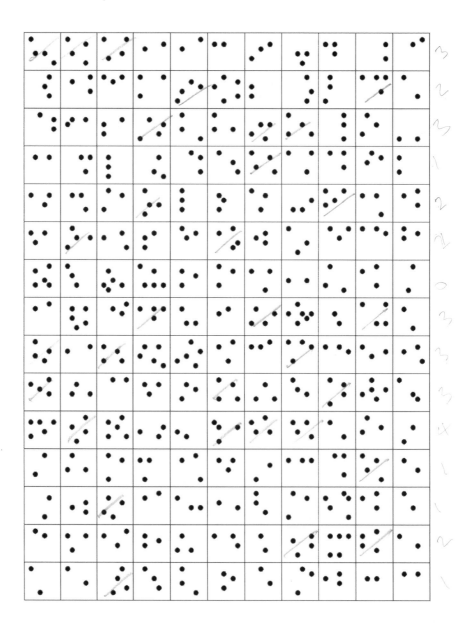

SAMPLE DOTS CONCENTRATION TEST 4

Place a diagonal line across each box that contains 4 dots only. You have 60 seconds to complete the test.

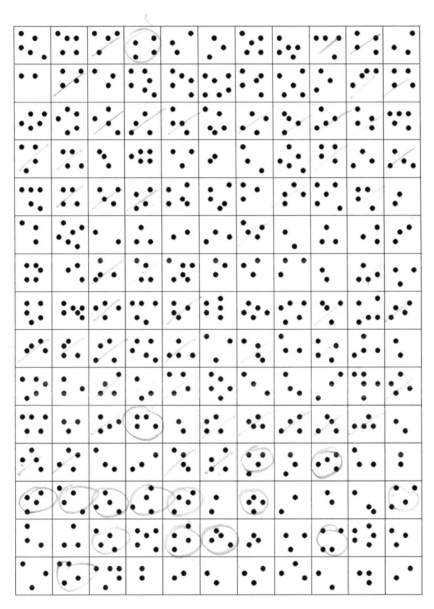

SAMPLE DOTS CONCENTRATION TEST 5

Place a diagonal line across each box that contains 4 dots only. You have 60 seconds to complete the test.

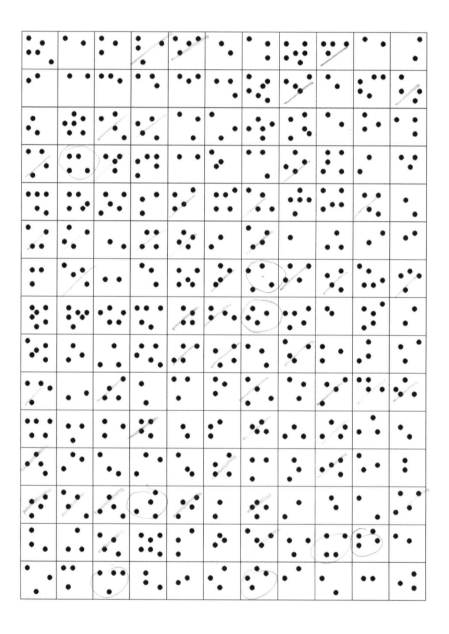

ANSWERS TO DOTS CONCENTRATION TESTS 1 TO 5

DOTS CONCENTRATION TEST 1

56 boxes containing groups of 4 dots

DOTS CONCENTRATION TEST 2

58 boxes containing groups of 4 dots

DOTS CONCENTRATION TEST 3

31 boxes containing groups of 4 dots

DOTS CONCENTRATION TEST 4

66 boxes containing groups of 4 dots

DOTS CONCENTRATION TEST 5

56 boxes containing groups of 4 dots

20 CONCENTRATION TESTS

I have now provided you with twenty sample Dots Concentration Tests. Each test consists of five pages of dots. You have just five minutes to complete each test, which equates to one minute per page of dots. I must stress that the time limit provided during these tests is not the same as the actual assessment. During the real test you will have little chance of completing it within the allotted time-frame.

Remember to work quickly and accurately. The answers to each test are provided at the end of the book.

DOTS
CONCENTRATION
TEST 1

DOTS CONCENTRATION TESTS

SHEET 1

Place a diagonal line across each box that contains 4 dots only.

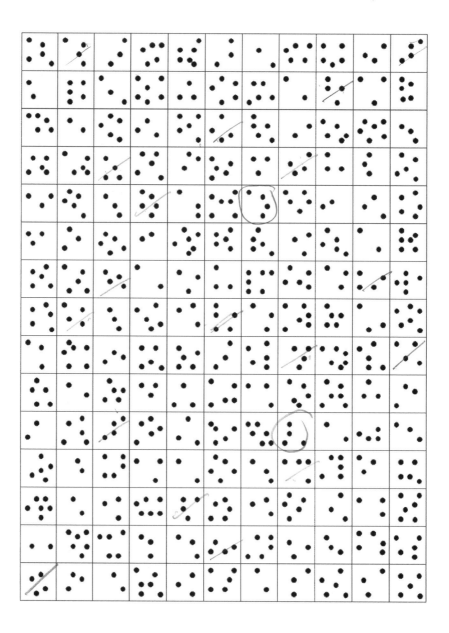

SHEET 2

Place a diagonal line across each box that contains 4 dots only.

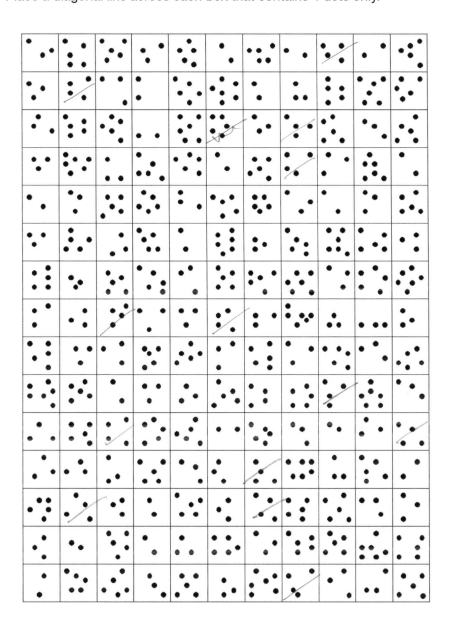

SHEET 3

Place a diagonal line across each box that contains 4 dots only.

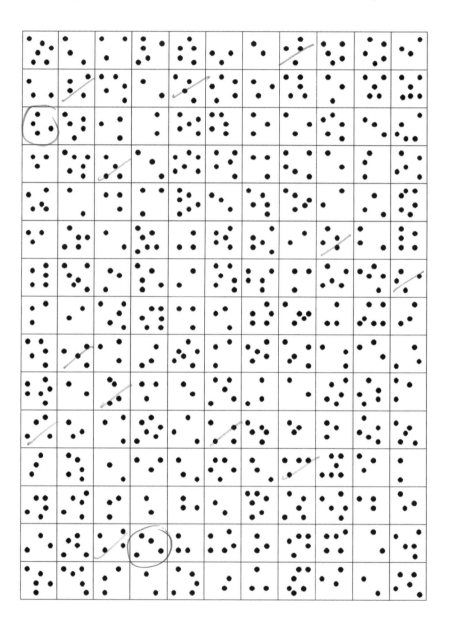

SHEET 4

Place a diagonal line across each box that contains 4 dots only.

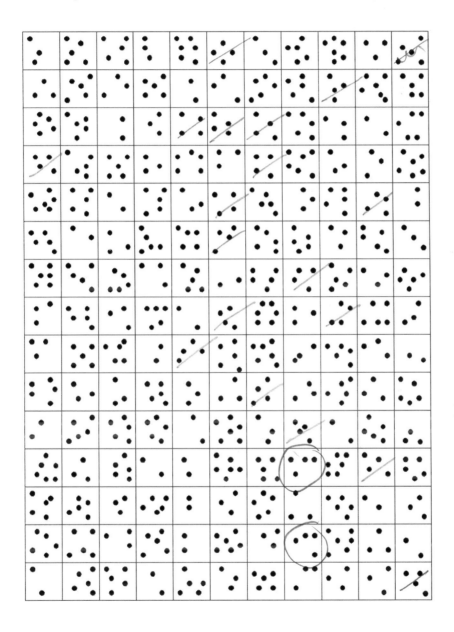

SHEET 5

Place a diagonal line across each box that contains 4 dots only.

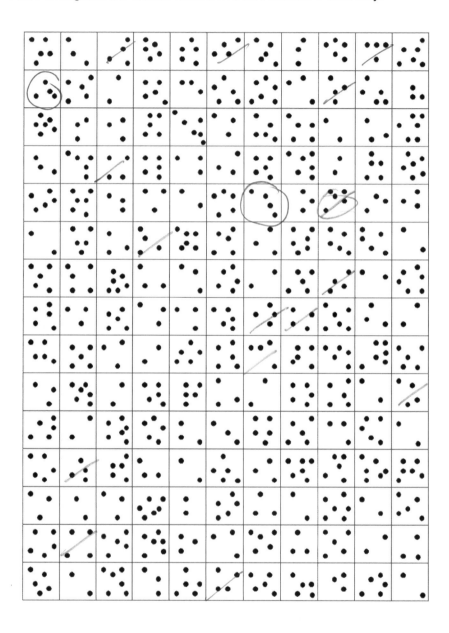

DOTS CONCENTRATION TEST 2

DOTS CONCENTRATION TESTS

SHEET 1

Place a diagonal line across each box that contains 4 dots only.

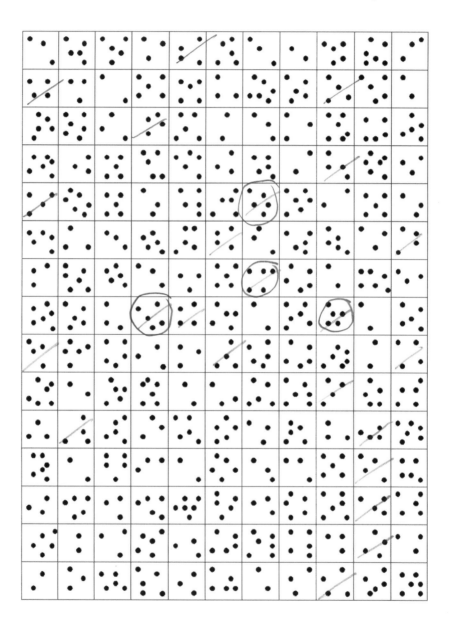

SHEET 2

Place a diagonal line across each box that contains 4 dots only.

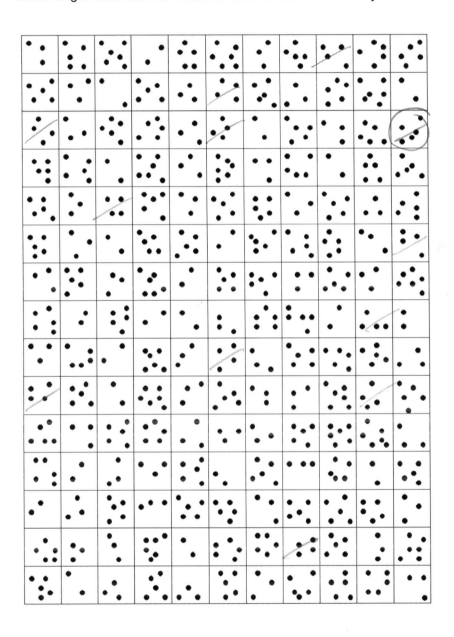

SHEET 3

Place a diagonal line across each box that contains 4 dots only.

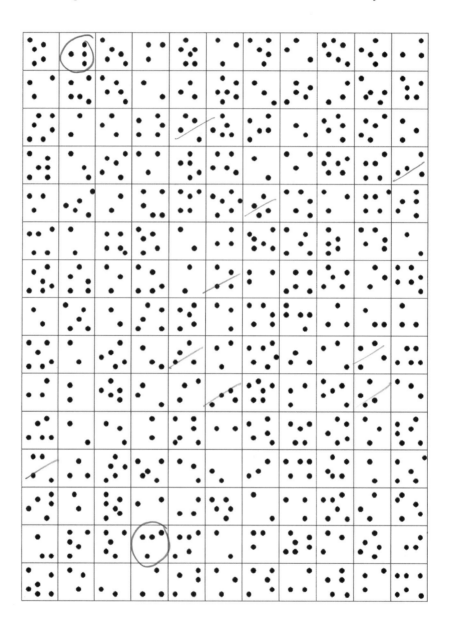

SHEET 4

Place a diagonal line across each box that contains 4 dots only.

SHEET 5

Place a diagonal line across each box that contains 4 dots only.

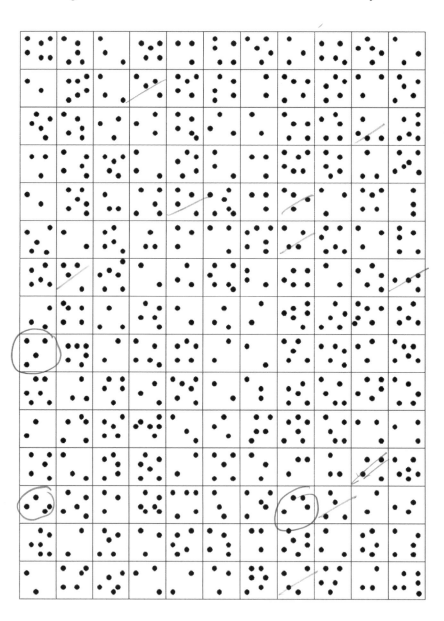

DOTS CONCENTRATION TEST 3

DOTS CONCENTRATION TESTS

SHEET 1

Place a diagonal line across each box that contains 4 dots only.

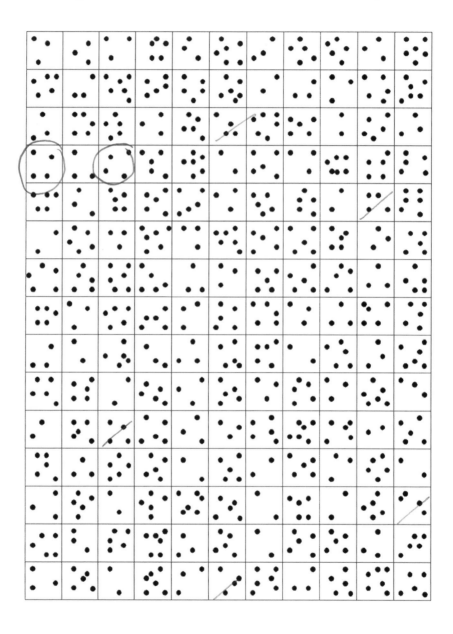

SHEET 2

Place a diagonal line across each box that contains 4 dots only.

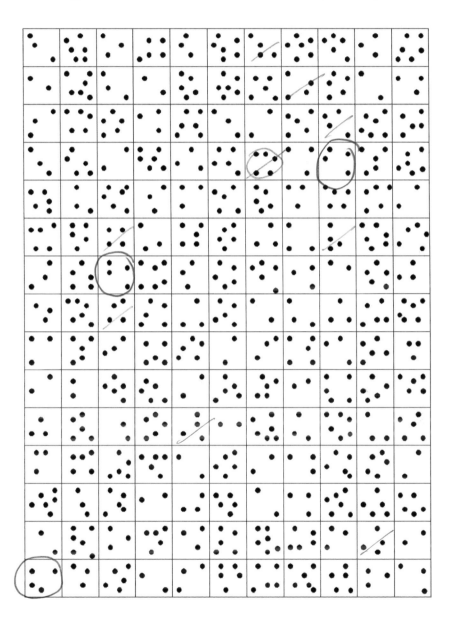

SHEET 3

Place a diagonal line across each box that contains 4 dots only.

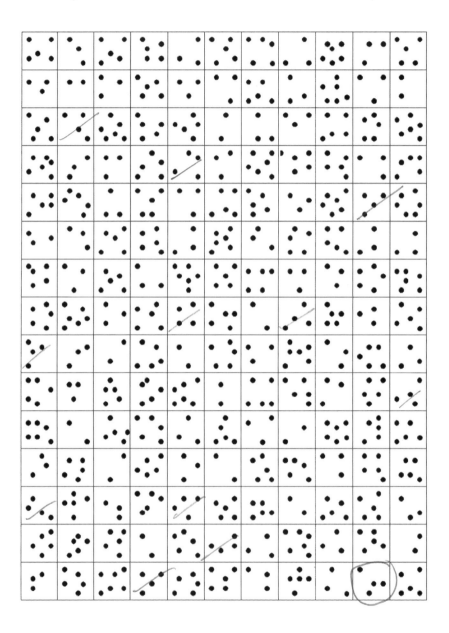

SHEET 4

Place a diagonal line across each box that contains 4 dots only.

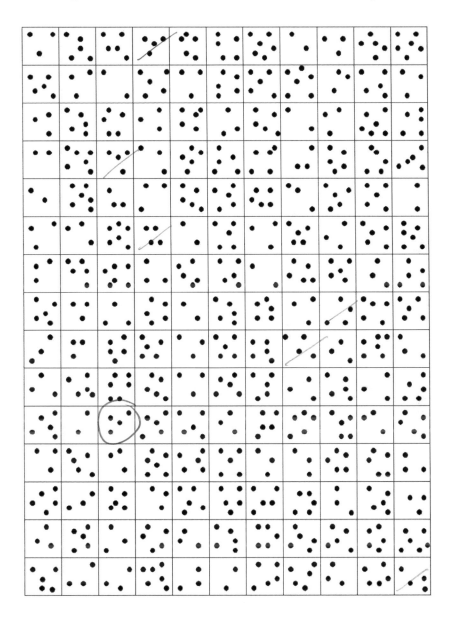

SHEET 5

Place a diagonal line across each box that contains 4 dots only.

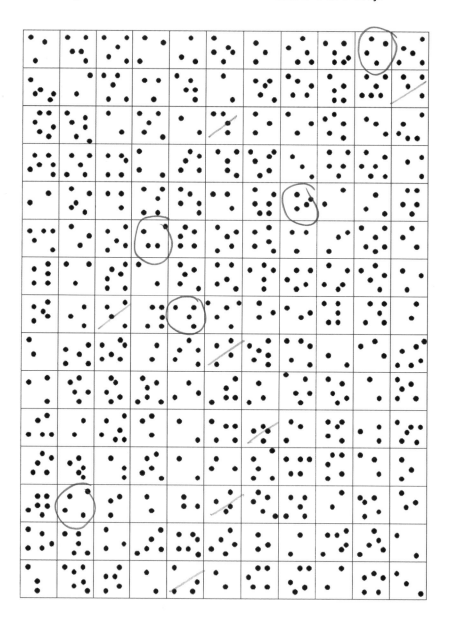

DOTS
CONCENTRATION
TEST 4

SHEET 1

Place a diagonal line across each box that contains 4 dots only.

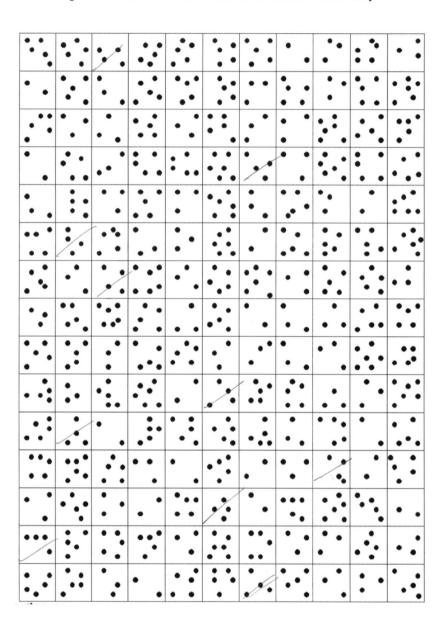

SHEET 2

Place a diagonal line across each box that contains 4 dots only.

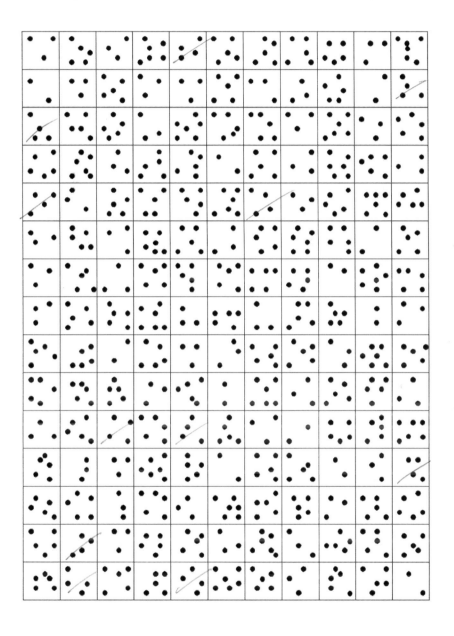

DOTS CONCENTRATION TESTS

SHEET 3

Place a diagonal line across each box that contains 4 dots only.

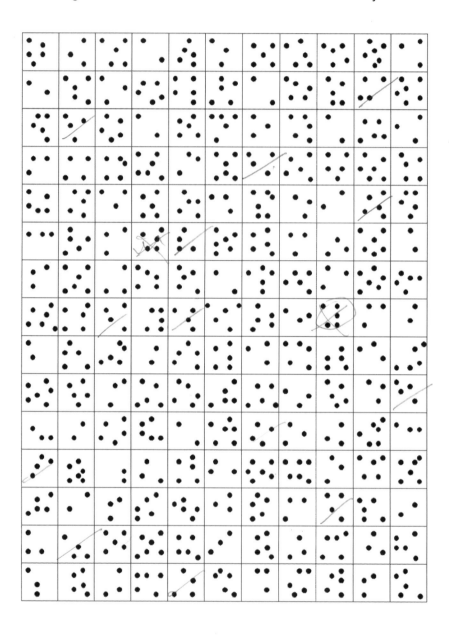

SHEET 4

Place a diagonal line across each box that contains 4 dots only.

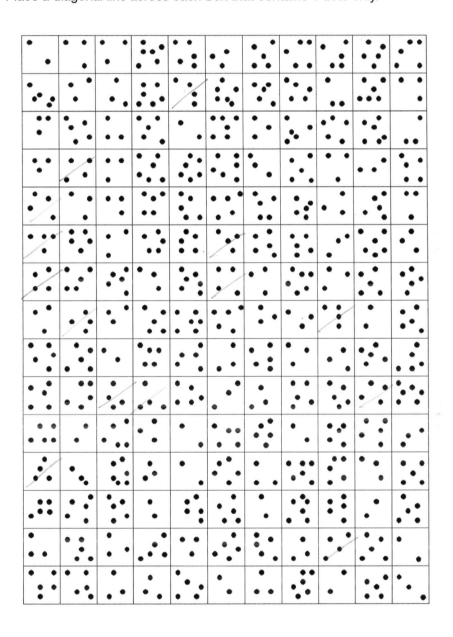

SHEET 5

Place a diagonal line across each box that contains 4 dots only.

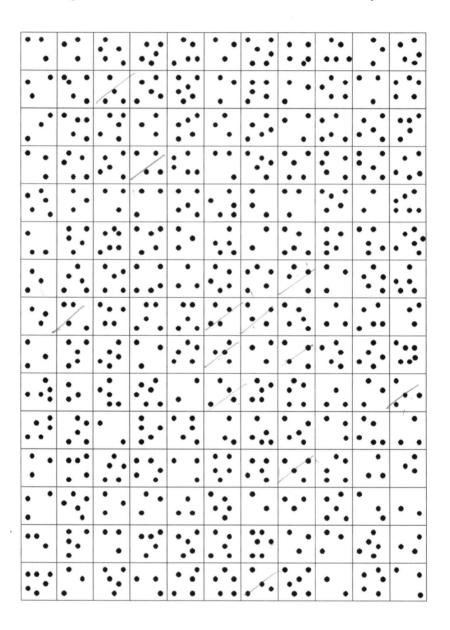

DOTS
CONCENTRATION
TEST 5

DOTS CONCENTRATION TESTS

SHEET 1

Place a diagonal line across each box that contains 4 dots only.

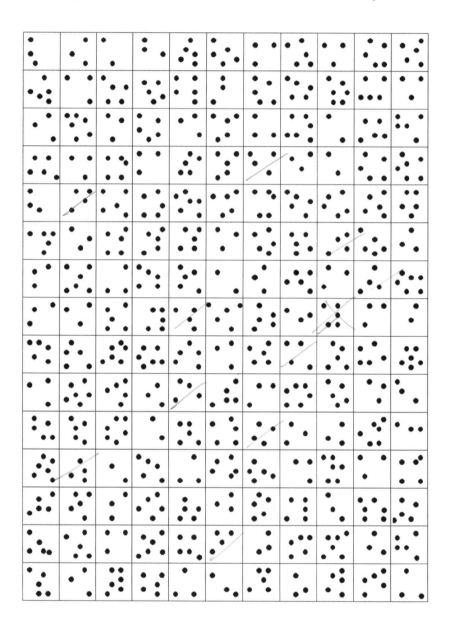

SHEET 2

Place a diagonal line across each box that contains 4 dots only.

SHEET 3

Place a diagonal line across each box that contains 4 dots only.

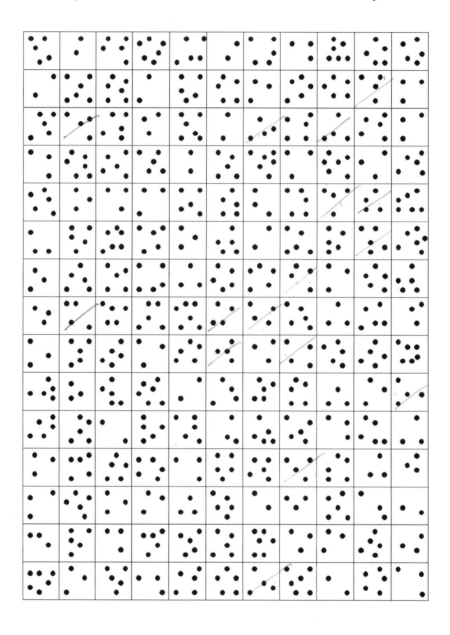

SHEET 4

Place a diagonal line across each box that contains 4 dots only.

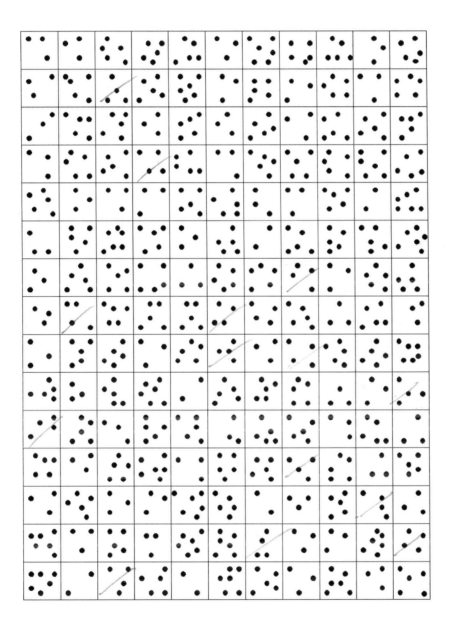

SHEET 5

Place a diagonal line across each box that contains 4 dots only.

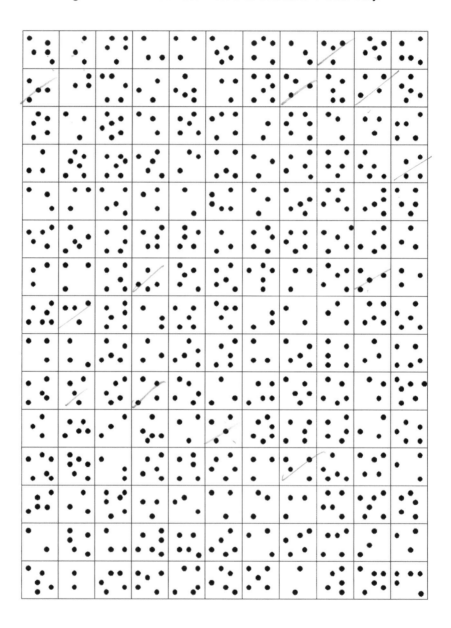

DOTS
CONCENTRATION
TEST 6

DOTS CONCENTRATION TESTS

SHEET 1

Place a diagonal line across each box that contains 4 dots only.

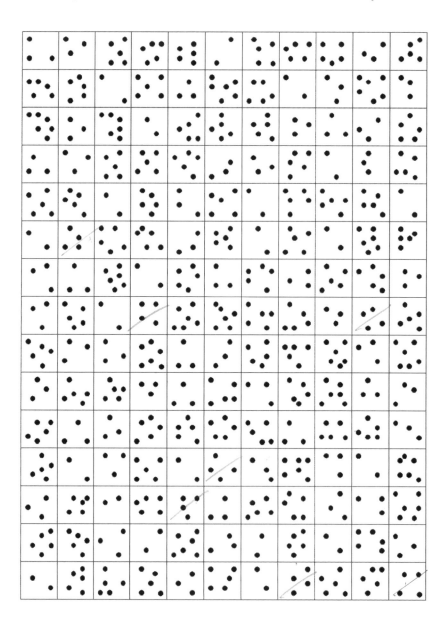

SHEET 2

Place a diagonal line across each box that contains 4 dots only.

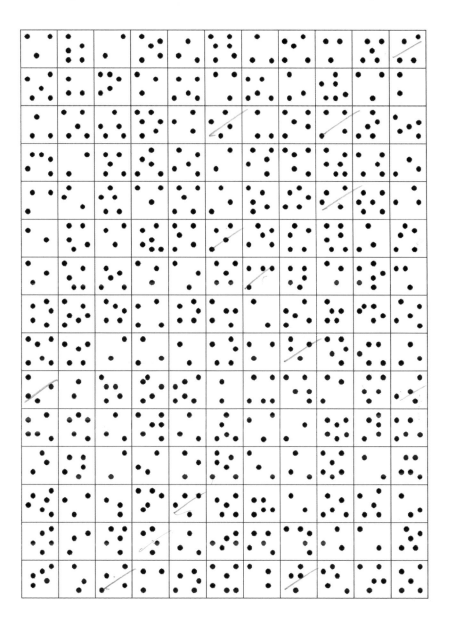

DOTS CONCENTRATION TESTS

SHEET 3

Place a diagonal line across each box that contains 4 dots only.

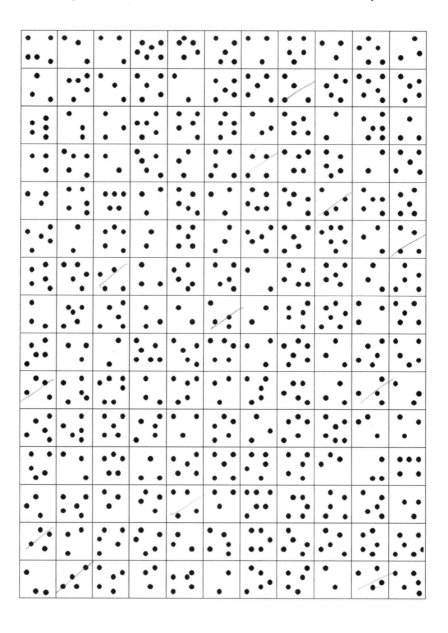

SHEET 4

Place a diagonal line across each box that contains 4 dots only.

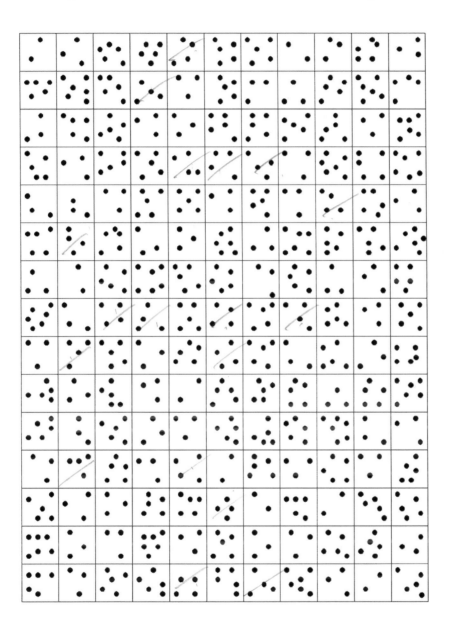

SHEET 5

Place a diagonal line across each box that contains 4 dots only.

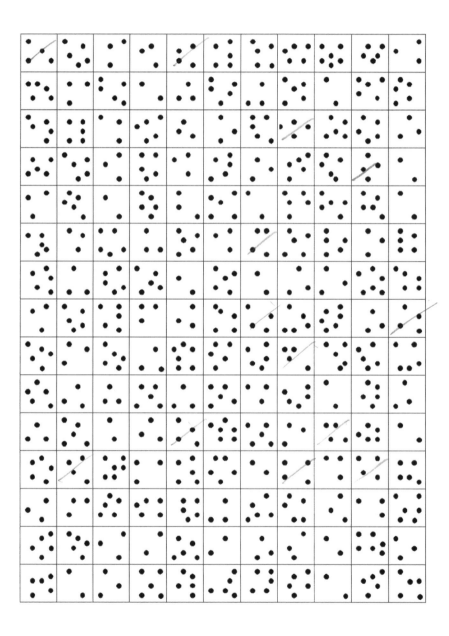

DOTS
CONCENTRATION
TEST 7

DOTS CONCENTRATION TESTS

SHEET 1

Place a diagonal line across each box that contains 4 dots only.

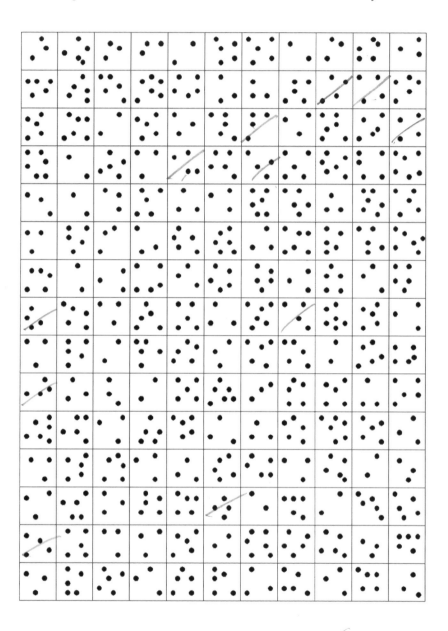

SHEET 2

Place a diagonal line across each box that contains 4 dots only.

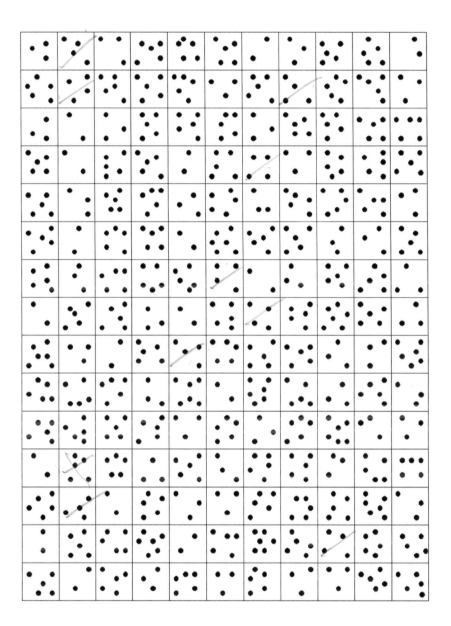

DOTS CONCENTRATION TESTS

SHEET 3

Place a diagonal line across each box that contains 4 dots only.

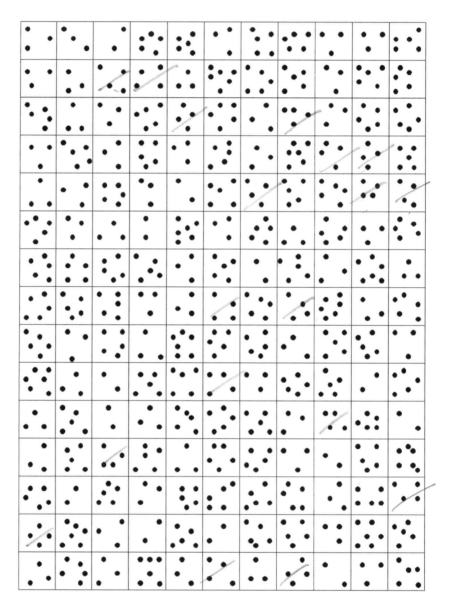

SHEET 4

Place a diagonal line across each box that contains 4 dots only.

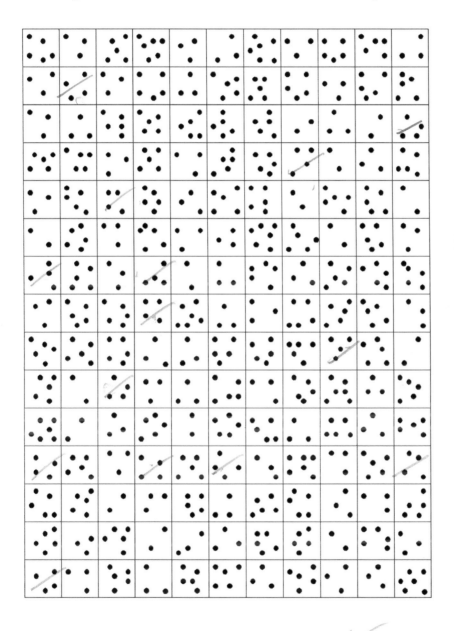

DOTS CONCENTRATION TESTS

SHEET 5

Place a diagonal line across each box that contains 4 dots only.

DOTS
CONCENTRATION
TEST 8

DOTS CONCENTRATION TESTS

SHEET 1

Place a diagonal line across each box that contains 4 dots only.

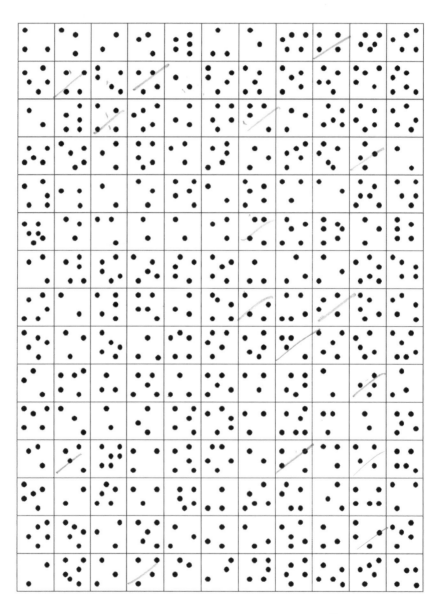

SHEET 2

Place a diagonal line across each box that contains 4 dots only.

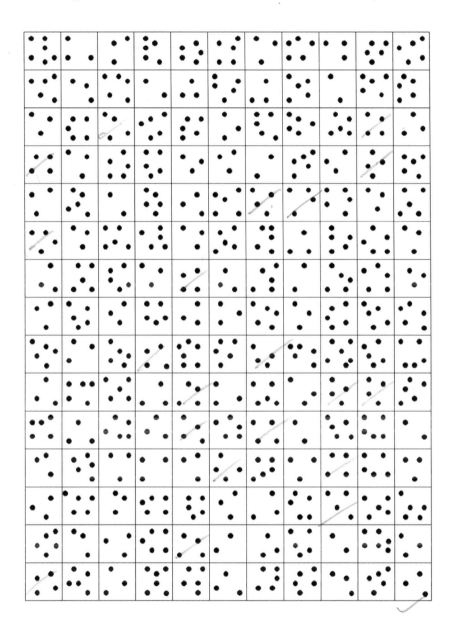

SHEET 3

Place a diagonal line across each box that contains 4 dots only.

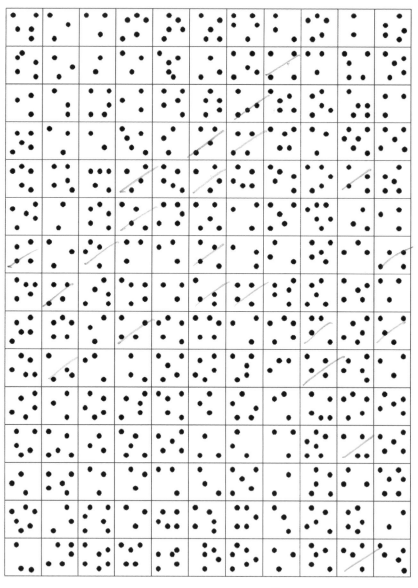

SHEET 4

Place a diagonal line across each box that contains 4 dots only.

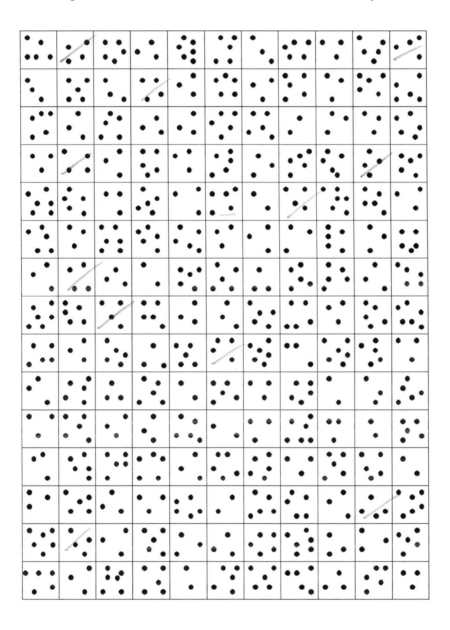

SHEET 5

Place a diagonal line across each box that contains 4 dots only.

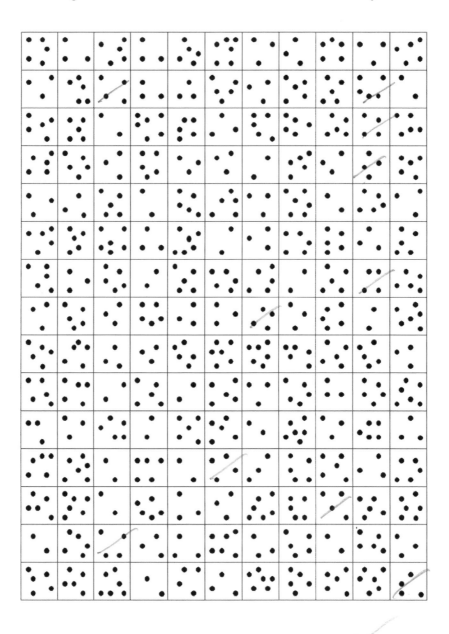

DOTS CONCENTRATION TEST 9

SHEET 1

Place a diagonal line across each box that contains 4 dots only.

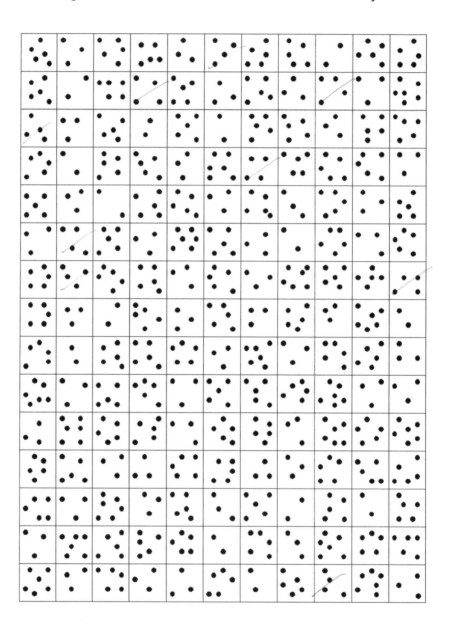

SHEET 2

Place a diagonal line across each box that contains 4 dots only.

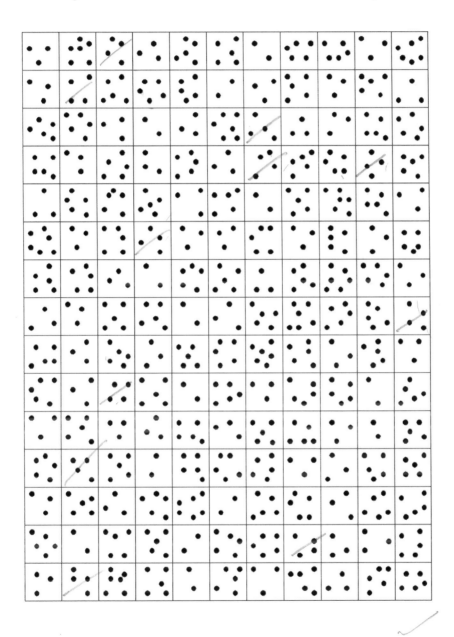

SHEET 3

Place a diagonal line across each box that contains 4 dots only.

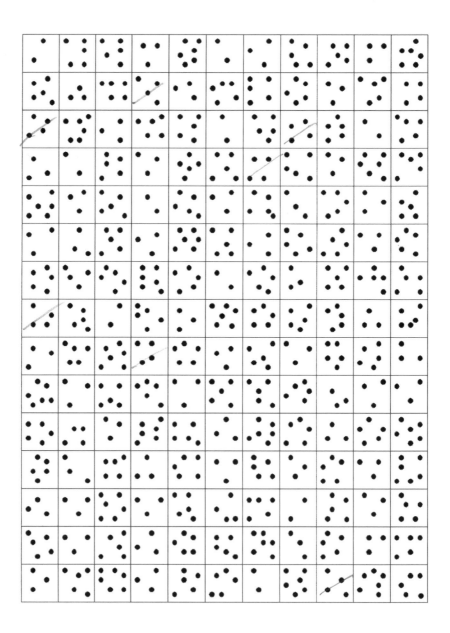

SHEET 4

Place a diagonal line across each box that contains 4 dots only.

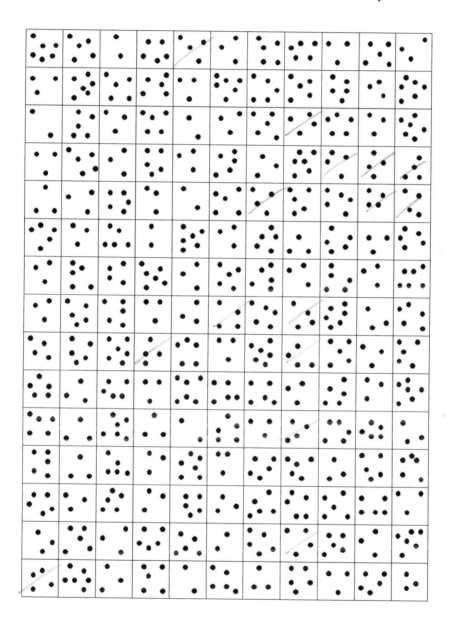

SHEET 5

Place a diagonal line across each box that contains 4 dots only.

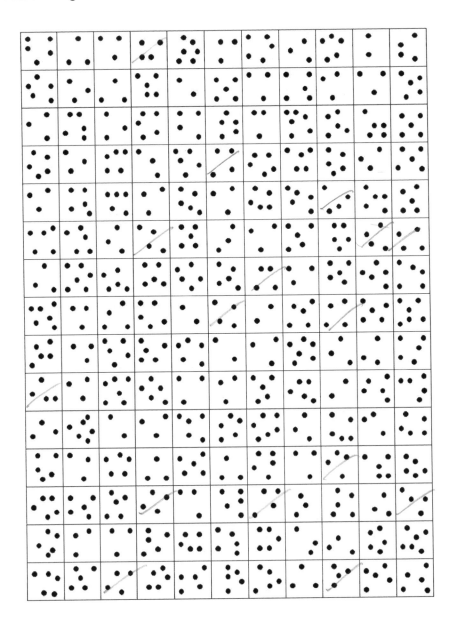

DOTS CONCENTRATION TEST 10

SHEET 1

Place a diagonal line across each box that contains 4 dots only.

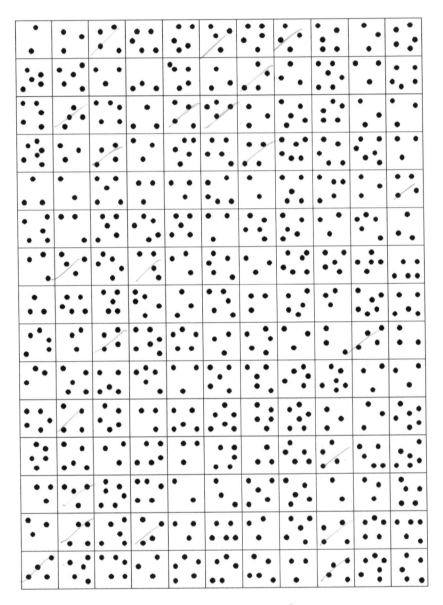

SHEET 2

Place a diagonal line across each box that contains 4 dots only.

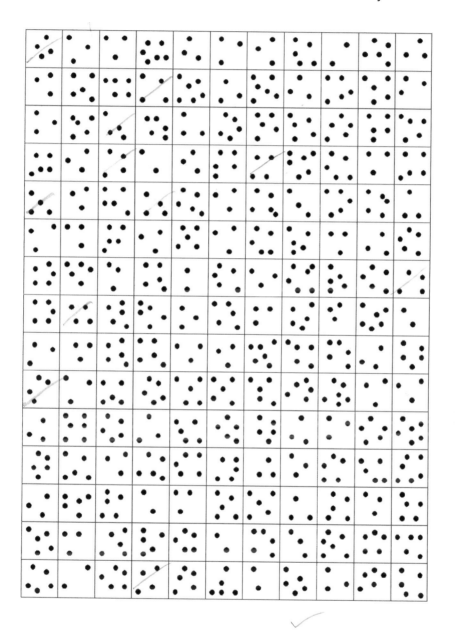

SHEET 3

Place a diagonal line across each box that contains 4 dots only.

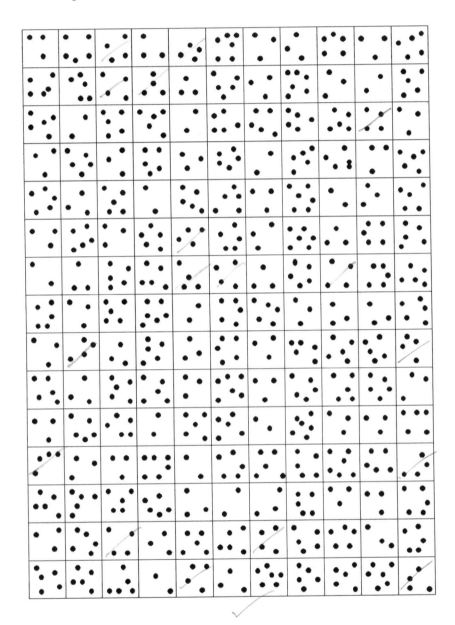

SHEET 4

Place a diagonal line across each box that contains 4 dots only.

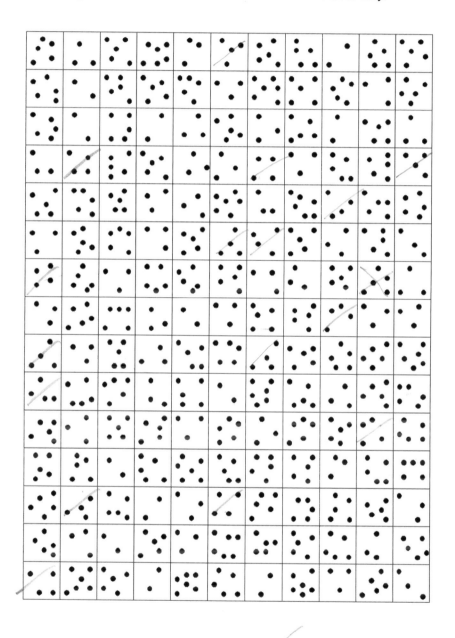

SHEET 5

Place a diagonal line across each box that contains 4 dots only.

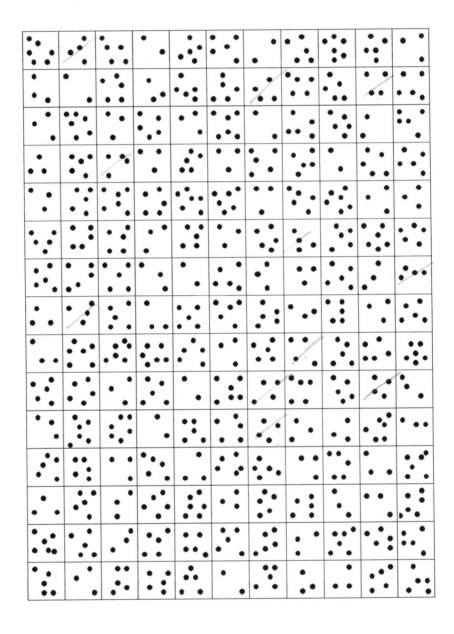

DOTS CONCENTRATION TEST 11

DOTS CONCENTRATION TESTS

SHEET 1

Place a diagonal line across each box that contains 4 dots only.

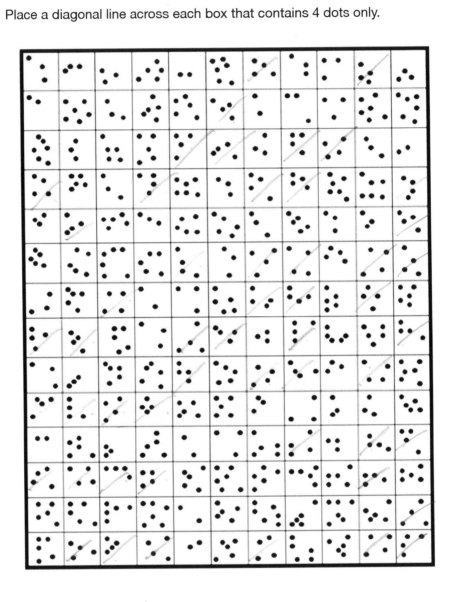

SHEET 2

Place a diagonal line across each box that contains 4 dots only.

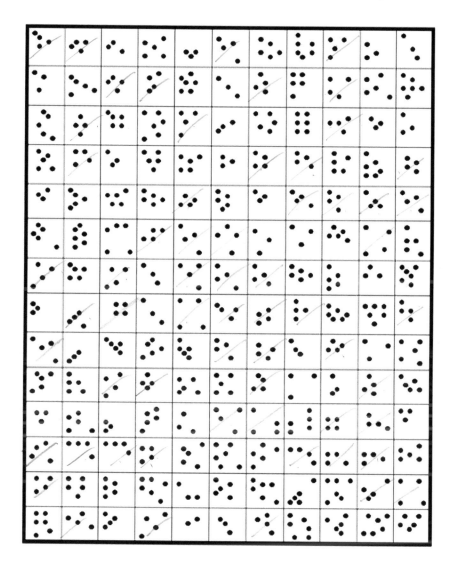

SHEET 3

Place a diagonal line across each box that contains 4 dots only.

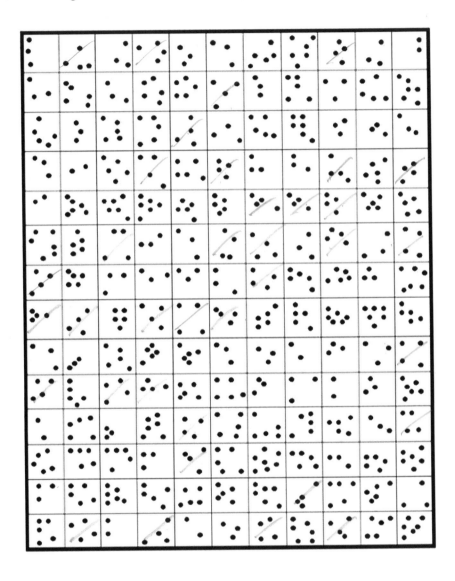

SHEET 4

Place a diagonal line across each box that contains 4 dots only.

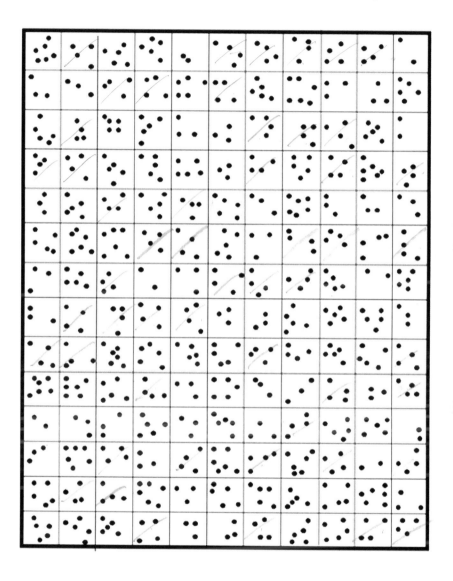

SHEET 5

Place a diagonal line across each box that contains 4 dots only.

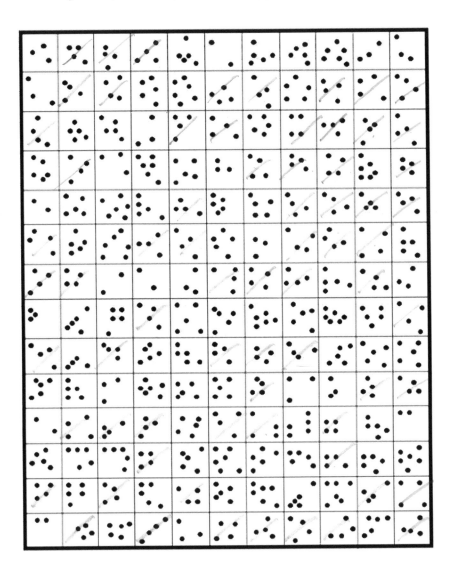

DOTS
CONCENTRATION
TEST 12

SHEET 1

Place a diagonal line across each box that contains 4 dots only.

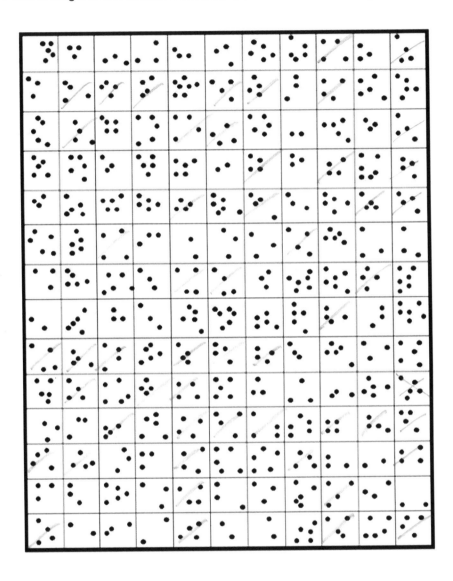

SHEET 2

Place a diagonal line across each box that contains 4 dots only.

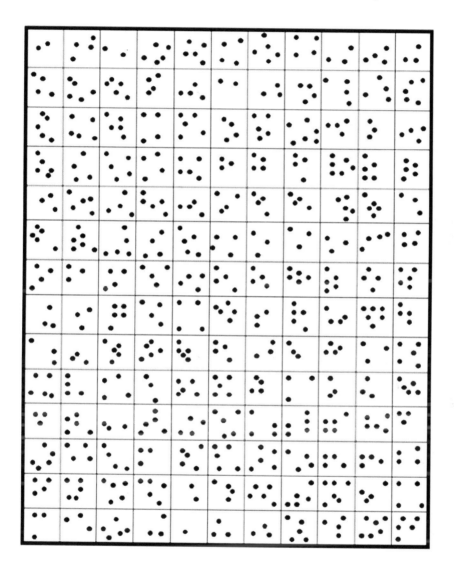

DOTS CONCENTRATION TESTS

SHEET 3

Place a diagonal line across each box that contains 4 dots only.

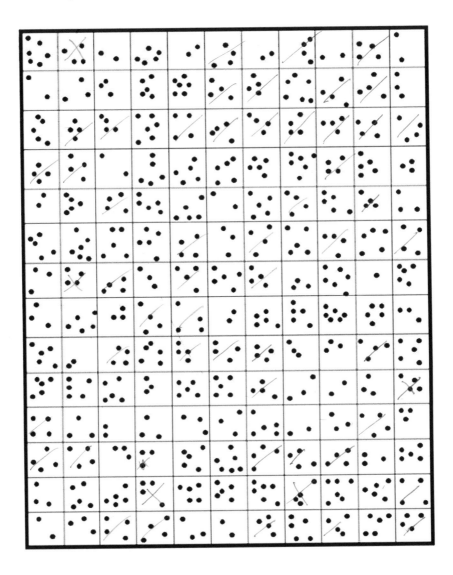

SHEET 4

Place a diagonal line across each box that contains 4 dots only.

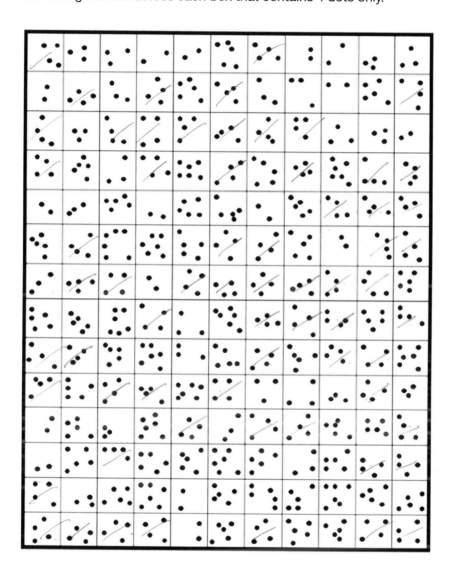

SHEET 5

Place a diagonal line across each box that contains 4 dots only.

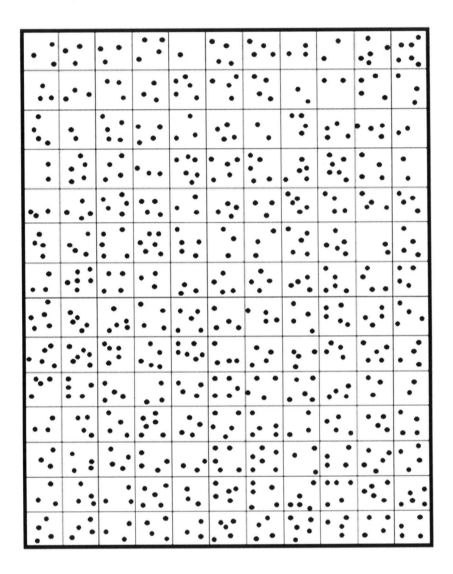

DOTS
CONCENTRATION
TEST 13

DOTS CONCENTRATION TESTS

SHEET 1

Place a diagonal line across each box that contains 4 dots only.

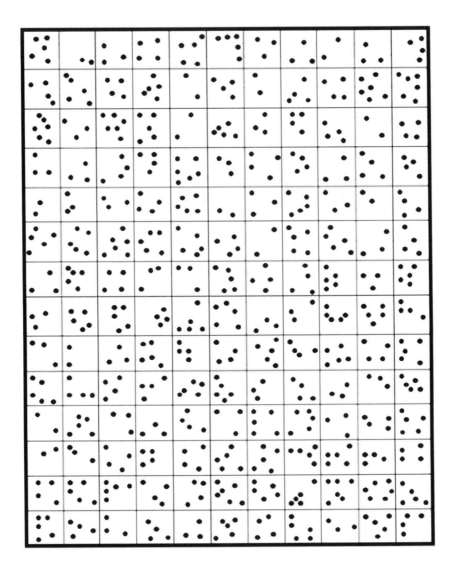

SHEET 2

Place a diagonal line across each box that contains 4 dots only.

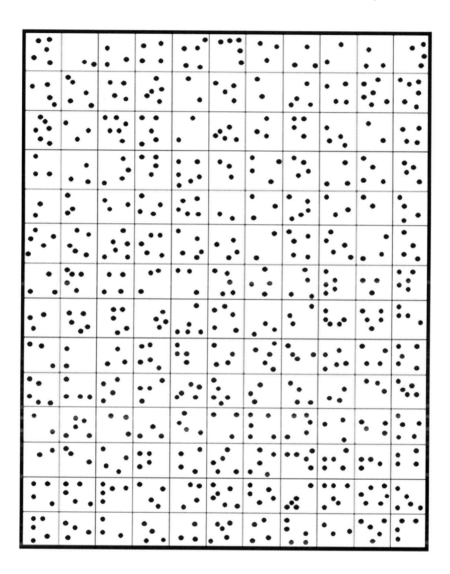

DOTS CONCENTRATION TESTS

SHEET 3

Place a diagonal line across each box that contains 4 dots only.

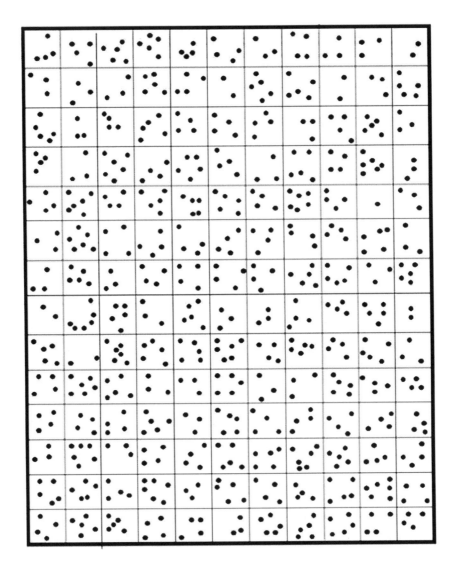

SHEET 4

Place a diagonal line across each box that contains 4 dots only.

DOTS CONCENTRATION TESTS

SHEET 5

Place a diagonal line across each box that contains 4 dots only.

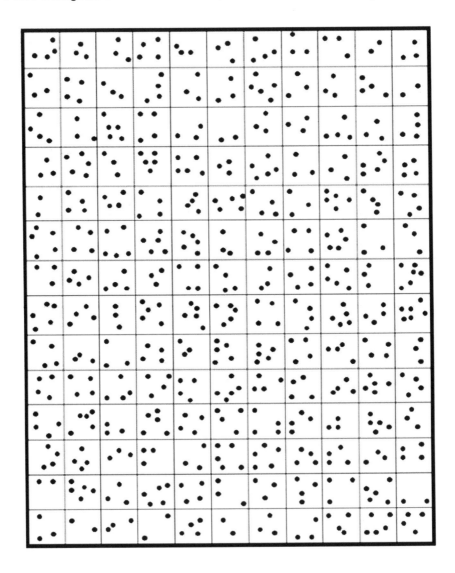

DOTS CONCENTRATION TEST 14

SHEET 1

Place a diagonal line across each box that contains 4 dots only.

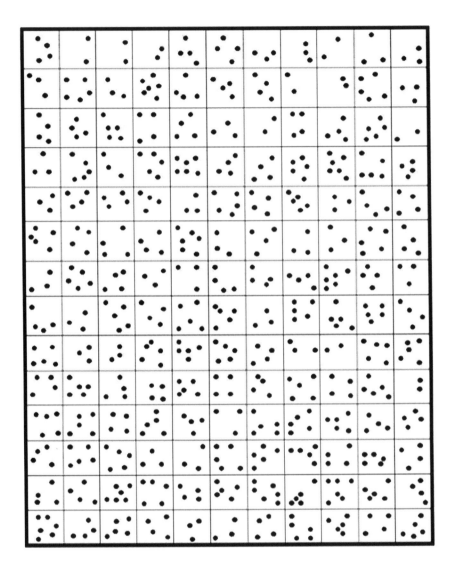

SHEET 2

Place a diagonal line across each box that contains 4 dots only.

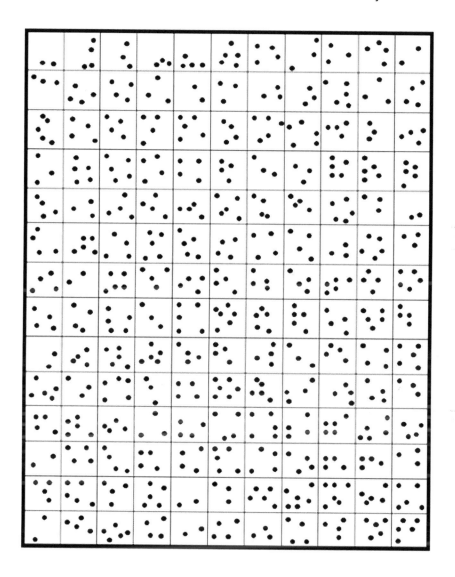

SHEET 3

Place a diagonal line across each box that contains 4 dots only.

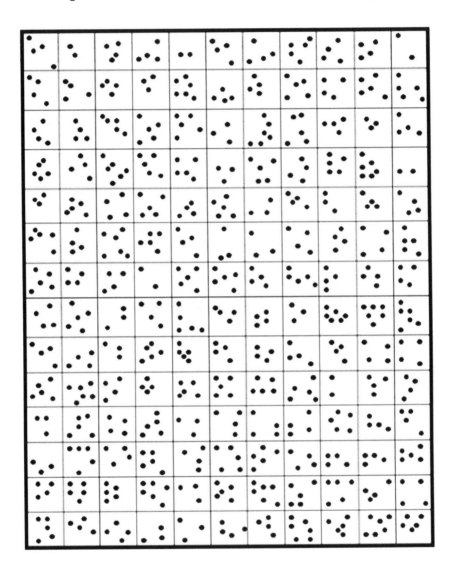

SHEET 4

Place a diagonal line across each box that contains 4 dots only.

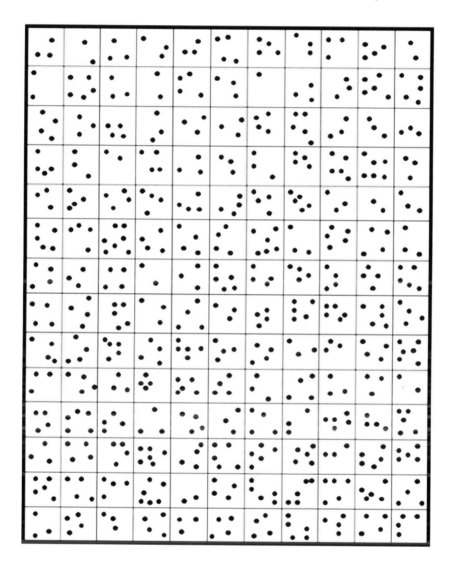

SHEET 5

Place a diagonal line across each box that contains 4 dots only.

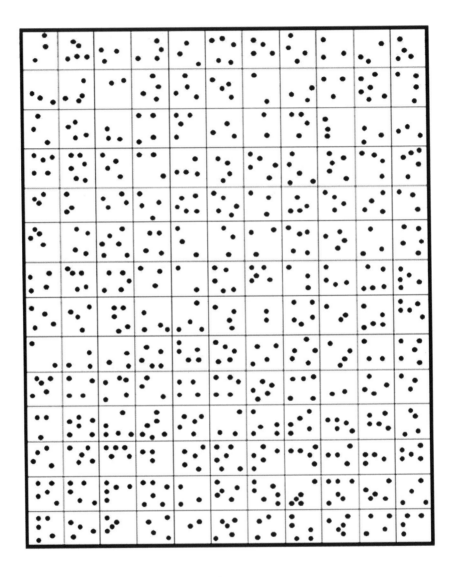

DOTS
CONCENTRATION
TEST 15

SHEET 1

Place a diagonal line across each box that contains 4 dots only.

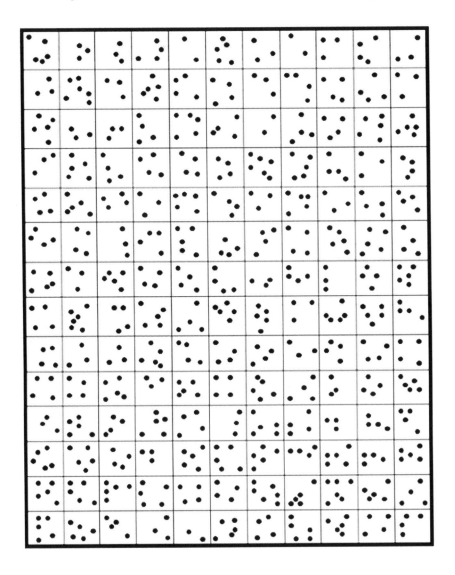

SHEET 2

Place a diagonal line across each box that contains 4 dots only.

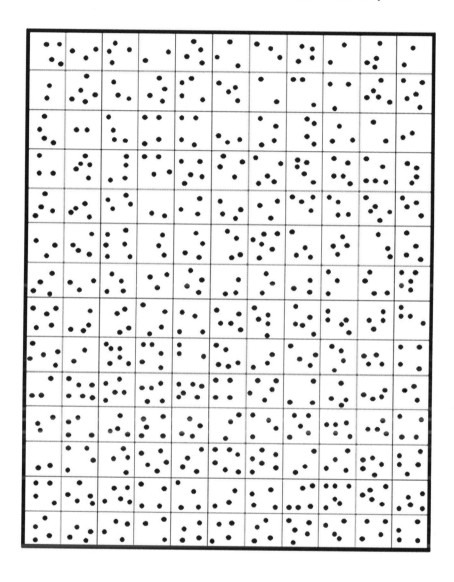

SHEET 3

Place a diagonal line across each box that contains 4 dots only.

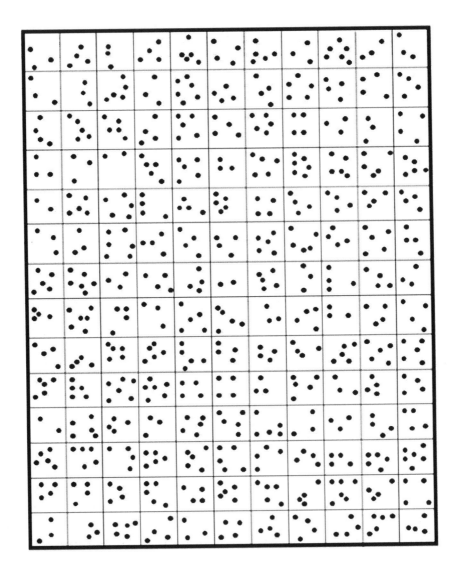

SHEET 4

Place a diagonal line across each box that contains 4 dots only.

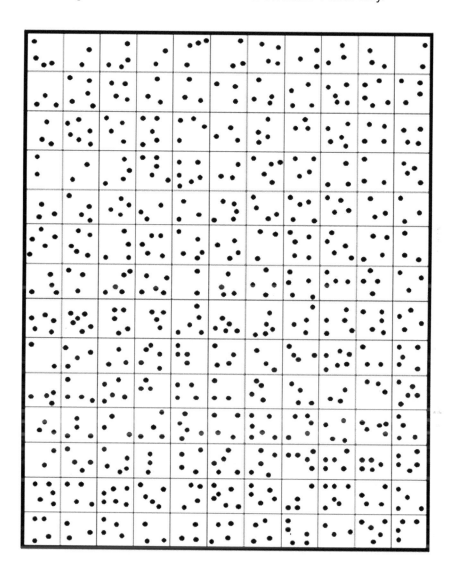

SHEET 5

Place a diagonal line across each box that contains 4 dots only.

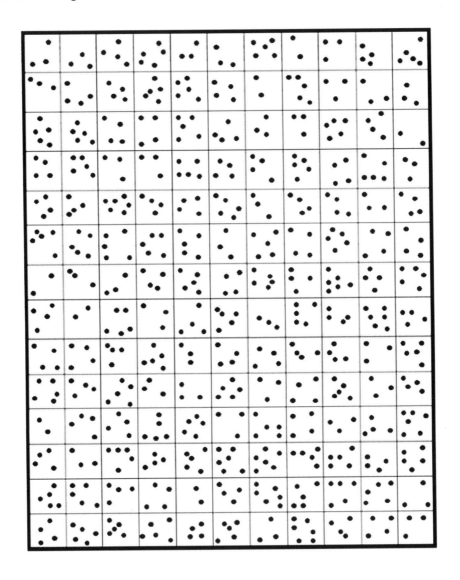

DOTS CONCENTRATION TEST 16

SHEET 1

Place a diagonal line across each box that contains 4 dots only.

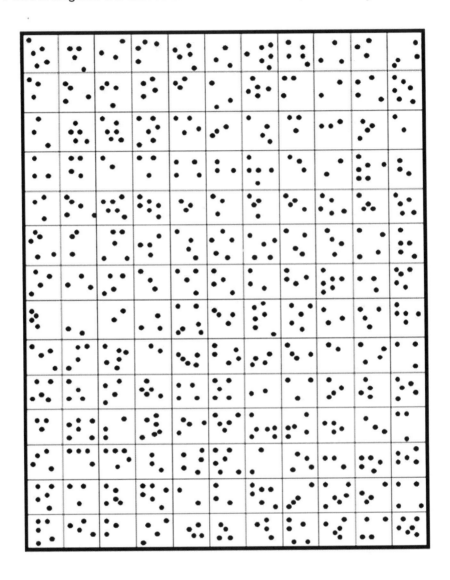

SHEET 2

Place a diagonal line across each box that contains 4 dots only.

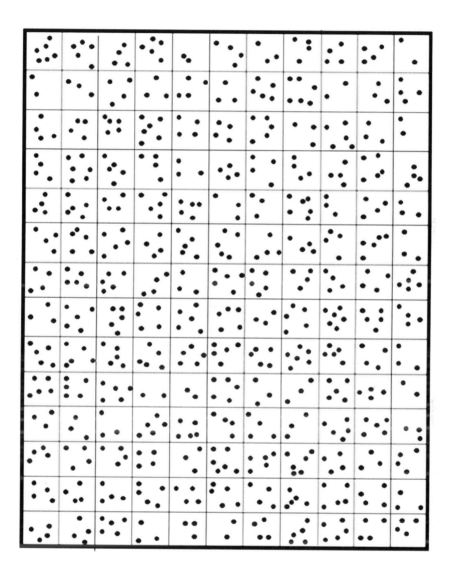

**DOTS CONCENTRATION
TESTS**

SHEET 3

Place a diagonal line across each box that contains 4 dots only.

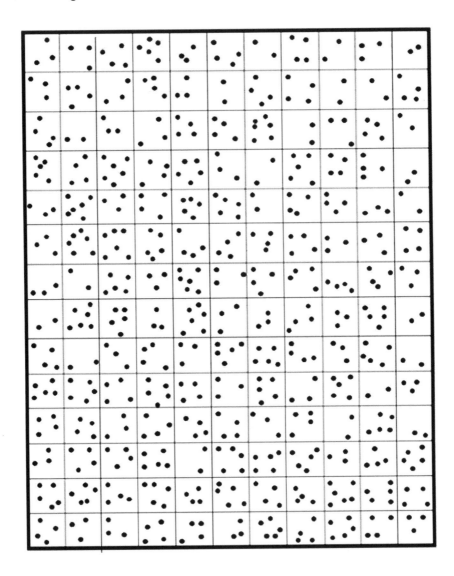

SHEET 4

Place a diagonal line across each box that contains 4 dots only.

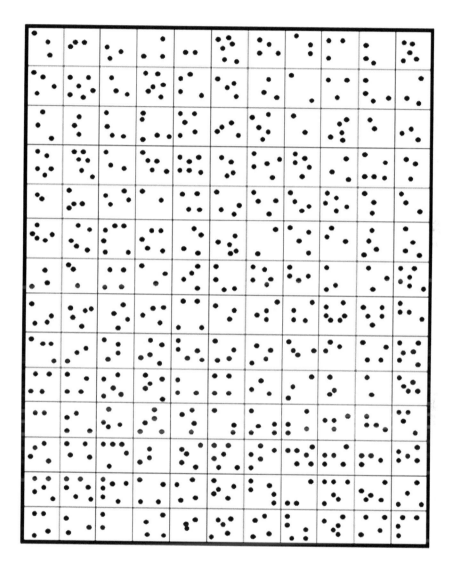

SHEET 5

Place a diagonal line across each box that contains 4 dots only.

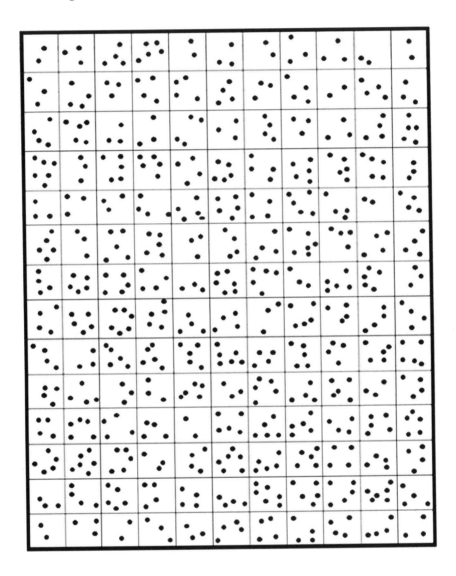

DOTS CONCENTRATION TEST 17

SHEET 1

Place a diagonal line across each box that contains 4 dots only.

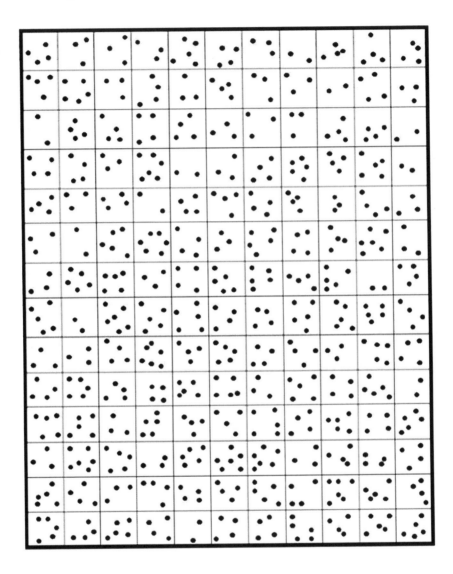

SHEET 2

Place a diagonal line across each box that contains 4 dots only.

SHEET 3

Place a diagonal line across each box that contains 4 dots only.

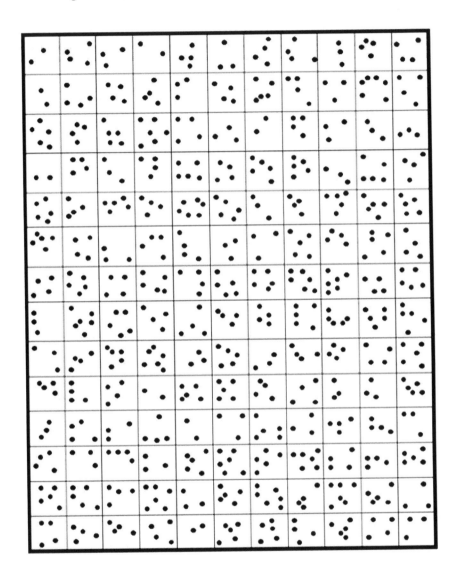

SHEET 4

Place a diagonal line across each box that contains 4 dots only.

SHEET 5

Place a diagonal line across each box that contains 4 dots only.

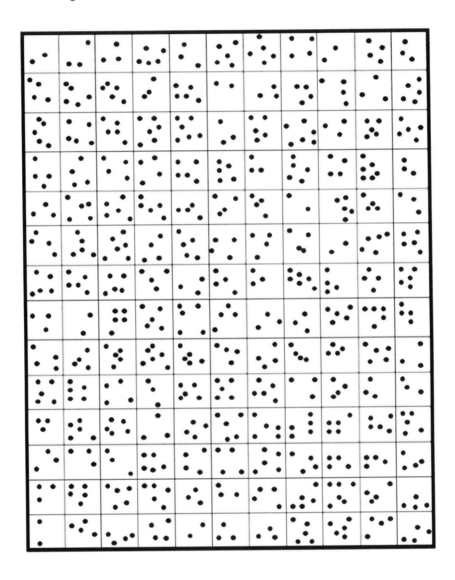

DOTS CONCENTRATION TEST 18

SHEET 1

Place a diagonal line across each box that contains 4 dots only.

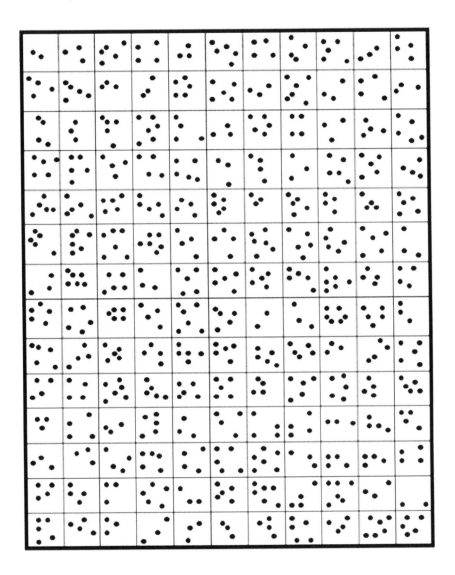

SHEET 2

Place a diagonal line across each box that contains 4 dots only.

SHEET 3

Place a diagonal line across each box that contains 4 dots only.

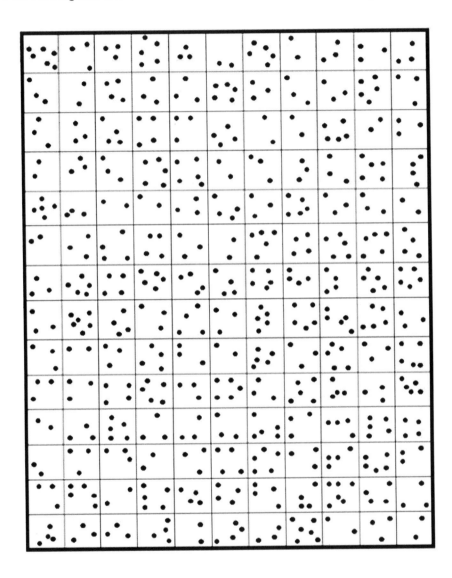

SHEET 4

Place a diagonal line across each box that contains 4 dots only.

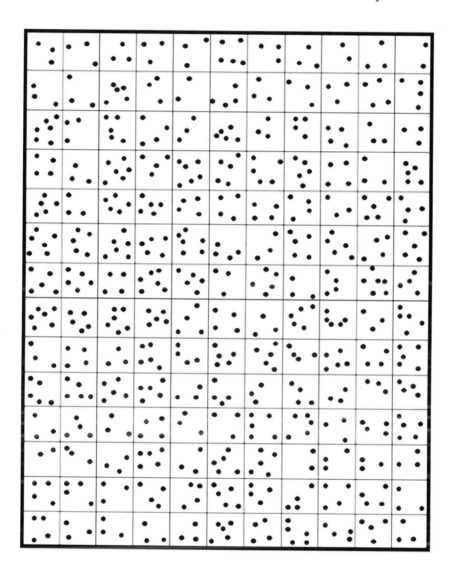

SHEET 5

Place a diagonal line across each box that contains 4 dots only.

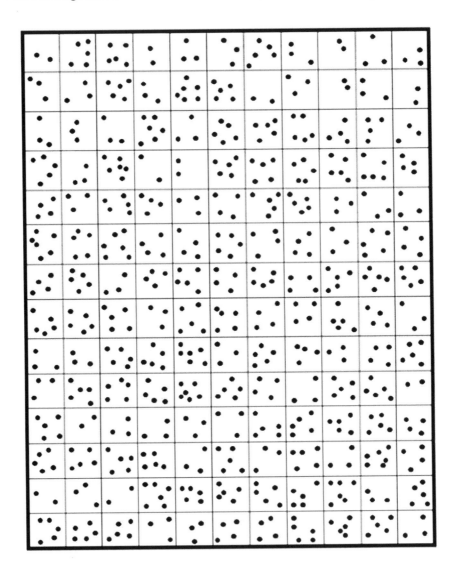

DOTS CONCENTRATION TEST 19

DOTS CONCENTRATION TESTS

SHEET 1

Place a diagonal line across each box that contains 4 dots only.

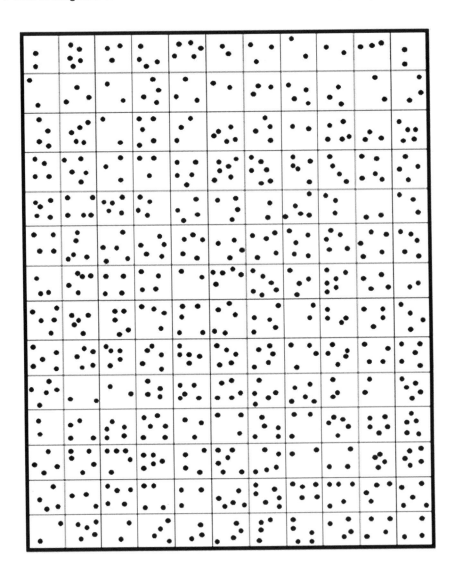

SHEET 2

Place a diagonal line across each box that contains 4 dots only.

SHEET 3

Place a diagonal line across each box that contains 4 dots only.

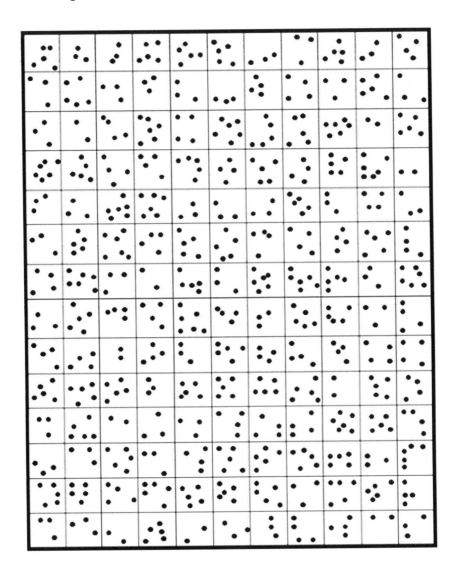

SHEET 4

Place a diagonal line across each box that contains 4 dots only.

SHEET 5

Place a diagonal line across each box that contains 4 dots only.

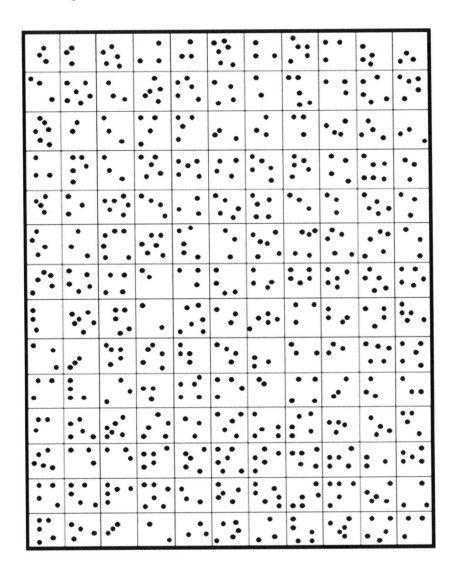

DOTS CONCENTRATION TEST 20

DOTS CONCENTRATION TESTS

SHEET 1

Place a diagonal line across each box that contains 4 dots only.

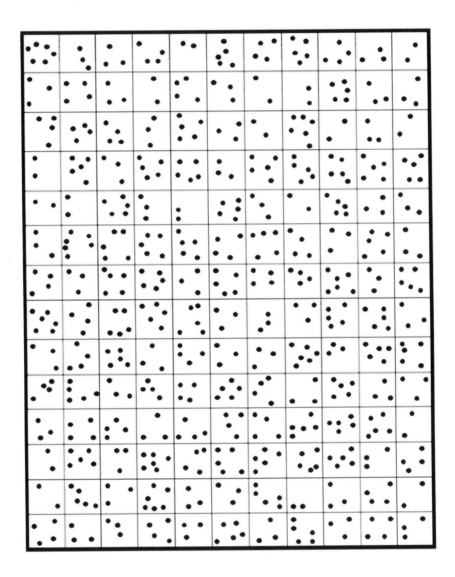

SHEET 2

Place a diagonal line across each box that contains 4 dots only.

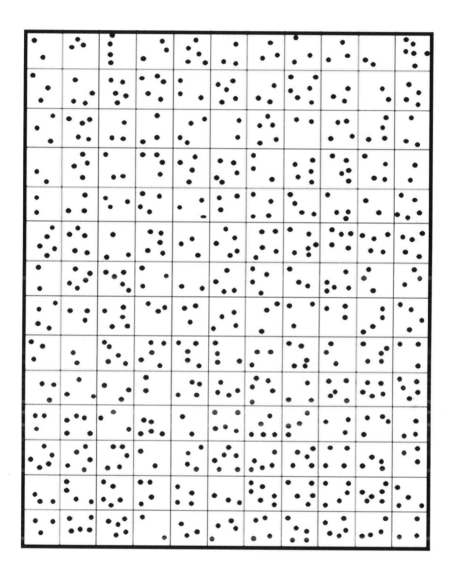

SHEET 3

Place a diagonal line across each box that contains 4 dots only.

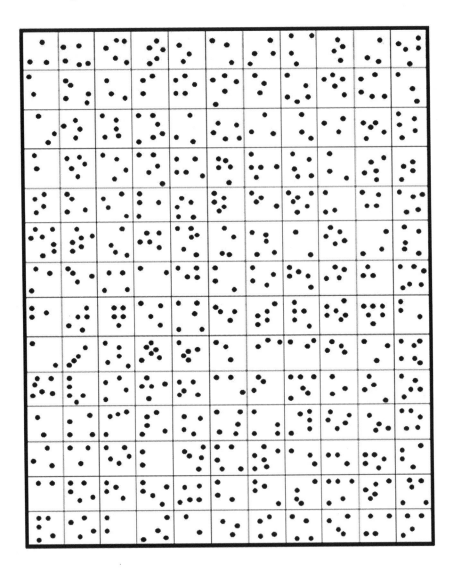

SHEET 4

Place a diagonal line across each box that contains 4 dots only.

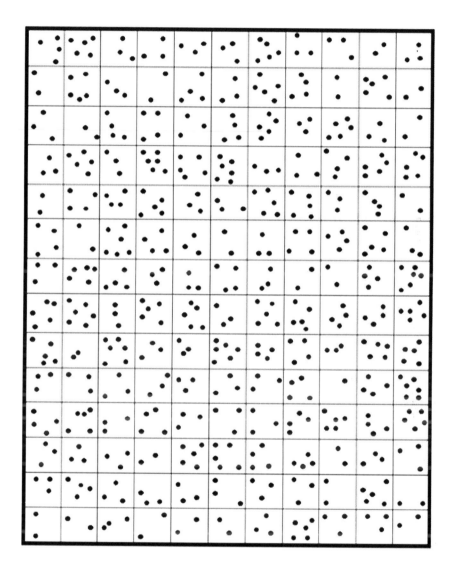

SHEET 5

Place a diagonal line across each box that contains 4 dots only.

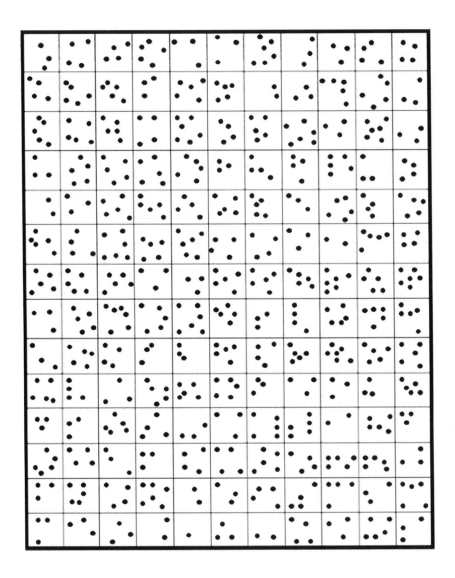

ANSWERS TO DOTS CONCENTRATION TESTS

DOTS CONCENTRATION TEST 1

Sheet 1 - 19

Sheet 2 - 14

Sheet 3 - 14

Sheet 4 - 20

Sheet 5 - 16

DOTS CONCENTRATION TEST 2

Sheet 1 - 19

Sheet 2 - 11

Sheet 3 - 11

Sheet 4 - 8

Sheet 5 - 13

DOTS CONCENTRATION TEST 3

Sheet 1 - 7

Sheet 2 - 11

Sheet 3 - 12

Sheet 4 - 7

Sheet 5 - 12

DOTS CONCENTRATION TEST 4

Sheet 1 - 10

Sheet 2 - 11

Sheet 3 - 13

Sheet 4 - 14

Sheet 5 - 12

DOTS CONCENTRATION TEST 5

Sheet 1 - 10

Sheet 2 - 11

Sheet 3 - 16

Sheet 4 - 15

Sheet 5 - 12

DOTS CONCENTRATION TEST 6

Sheet 1 - 7

Sheet 2 - 14

Sheet 3 - 13

Sheet 4 - 19

Sheet 5 - 13

DOTS CONCENTRATION TEST 7

Sheet 1 - 11

Sheet 2 - 9

Sheet 3 - 18

Sheet 4 - 14

Sheet 5 - 12

DOTS CONCENTRATION TEST 8

Sheet 1 - 16

Sheet 2 - 20

Sheet 3 - 22

Sheet 4 - 11

Sheet 5 - 10

DOTS CONCENTRATION TEST 9

Sheet 1 - 9

Sheet 2 - 11

Sheet 3 - 11

Sheet 4 - 17

Sheet 5 - 19

DOTS CONCENTRATION TEST 10

Sheet 1 - 22

Sheet 2 - 11

Sheet 3 - 17

Sheet 4 - 16

Sheet 5 - 11

DOTS CONCENTRATION TEST 11

Sheet 1 - 53

Sheet 2 - 62

Sheet 3 - 36

Sheet 4 - 54

Sheet 5 - 70

DOTS CONCENTRATION TEST 12

Sheet 1 - 52

Sheet 2 - 56

Sheet 3 - 55

Sheet 4 - 65

Sheet 5 - 64

DOTS CONCENTRATION TESTS

DOTS CONCENTRATION TEST 13

Sheet 1 - 47

Sheet 2 - 47

Sheet 3 - 58

Sheet 4 - 60

Sheet 5 - 59

DOTS CONCENTRATION TEST 14

Sheet 1 - 56

Sheet 2 - 69

Sheet 3 - 69

Sheet 4 - 61

Sheet 5 - 49

DOTS CONCENTRATION TEST 15

Sheet 1 - 65

Sheet 2 - 71

Sheet 3 - 63

Sheet 4 - 57

Sheet 5 - 55

DOTS CONCENTRATION TEST 16

Sheet 1 - 52

Sheet 2 - 54

Sheet 3 - 53

Sheet 4 - 56

Sheet 5 - 55

DOTS CONCENTRATION TEST 17

Sheet 1 - 62

Sheet 2 - 49

Sheet 3 - 60

Sheet 4 - 38

Sheet 5 - 48

DOTS CONCENTRATION TEST 18

Sheet 1 - 46

Sheet 2 - 45

Sheet 3 - 32

Sheet 4 - 43

Sheet 5 - 25

DOTS CONCENTRATION TEST 19

Sheet 1 - 36

Sheet 2 - 42

Sheet 3 - 38

Sheet 4 - 39

Sheet 5 - 26

DOTS CONCENTRATION TEST 20

Sheet 1 - 31

Sheet 2 - 35

Sheet 3 - 41

Sheet 4 - 30

Sheet 5 - 30

A FEW FINAL WORDS

You have now reached the end of the guide, and I hope that you have found it a useful tool in helping you to prepare for concentration tests. It is important that you remember the following tips:

Tip 1 – You will be assessed against both speed and accuracy. If you select groups of dots other than groups of four, you will lose marks. Aim for consistency.

Tip 2 – Do not worry if you cannot complete a sheet of dots. The test is designed so that you are unable to finish it.

Tip 3 – If you feel your eyes becoming tired, take a few seconds break before moving on to the next sheet. Just by resting your eyes for a few seconds you should find that this improves your concentration.

Tip 4 – The only way to improve your scores is to carry out lots of practice. You can try out more tests at the following website:

WWW.TRAINDRIVERTESTS.CO.UK

how2become

Visit www.how2become.com to find more titles and courses that will help you to pass the Train Driver selection process, including:

- **How to become a Train Driver.**

- **1-day Train Driver training course.**

- **Online testing suite.**

- **Psychometric testing books and CD's.**

www.how2become.com

Printed in Great Britain
by Amazon